CLERGY CONFERENCES — Canon 131

THE CATHOLIC UNIVERSITY OF AMERICA
CANON LAW STUDIES
No. 383

CLERGY CONFERENCES
Canon 131

A HISTORICAL CONSPECTUS
AND A CANONICAL COMMENTARY

A DISSERTATION

Submitted to the Faculty of the School of Canon Law of the Catholic University of America in Partial Fulfillment of the Requirements for the Degree of Doctor of Canon Law

BY

LAWRENCE JOSEPH HOFFMAN, A.B., S.T.B., J.C.L.
Priest of the Diocese of Sioux City, Iowa

THE CATHOLIC UNIVERSITY OF AMERICA PRESS
WASHINGTON, D. C.
1957

Nihil Obstat:

EDUARDUS ROELKER, S.T.D., J.C.D.,
Censor Deputatus.

Washingtonii, D. C., die 17 maii, 1957.

Imprimatur:

✠ JOSEPHUS M. MUELLER, D.D.,
Episcopus Sioupolitanus.

Siopoli, die 20 maii, 1957.

Printed by
THE WICKERSHAM PRINTING CO.
Lancaster, Pennsylvania

TO MY MOTHER AND FATHER

FOREWORD

The primary end of the Catholic Church as a perfect society is the eternal salvation of the souls of its members. It is for this reason that the Church has ever been very solicitous about the clergy, to whose charge the souls of the faithful are entrusted. The institute known as Clergy Conferences has played a significant role in preserving and furthering the competence and efficiency of the ministers of Chirst.

The present treatise restricts the history and canonical commentary of the conferences to the priests mentioned in canon 131 of the present Code of Canon Law. The canon includes all secular priests, religious, even exempt, who have the care of souls, and religious confessors who do not attend the conferences in their own houses. Responses given by the Sacred Congregation of the Holy Office and the Commission for the Authentic Interpretation of the Code indicate that all such clergymen must attend and participate in the diocesan conferences.

In examining the historical aspects of the institute, the present writer has found little on record about it before the time of Saint Charles Borromeo. This does not indicate that laws were not enacted concerning it before the time of Saint Charles, for there is evidence of occasional references to such enactments. Accordingly most of the matter will be concerned with clergy conferences from the time of Saint Charles to the present universal legislation of the Code of Canon Law.

The first chapter treats of the definition and beginnings of the institute. Enactments and the comparatively few references before the Council of Trent are comprised in the second chapter. The third chapter deals with the main influences upon the institute, especially the important impetus given it by Saint Charles Borromeo and the significance of the Tuesday conferences of Saint Vincent de Paul. The fourth chapter takes in the history of the institute from the Council of Rome (1725) to the present Code of Canon Law.

The canonical commentary treats the notion, purpose and subject-matter of the conferences in the fifth chapter. The sixth chapter explores the organization of the conferences with reference to the enactments of the III Plenary Council of Baltimore. The seventh chapter treats under various aspects the ordinary's obligation of convening and the clergy's duty of attending the conferences. Again, the legislation of the III Plenary Council of Baltimore is compared with the present universal law. The final chapter briefly deals with the penal sanction for the obligatory attendance at the conferences in accord with the norms established in canon 2377.

The writer wishes to express his filial gratitude to his Bishop, the Most Revered Joseph M. Mueller, Ordinary of the diocese of Sioux City, Iowa, for the opportunity of advanced study in Canon Law. He likewise wishes to thank the members of the Faculty of the School of Canon Law, his classmates of the University and all who have aided in any way in the preparation of dissertation.

TABLE OF CONTENTS

CHAPTER VI

CHAPTER VII

CHAPTER VIII

PART I

HISTORICAL CONSPECTUS

CHAPTER I

DEFINITION AND BEGINNINGS OF THE INSTITUTE KNOWN AS CLERGY CONFERENCES

Clergy conferences, as the term will be employed in the pages of this treatise, refer only to a very particular type of clerical gathering. Therefore, it is necessary to formulate an accurate definition of this institute as found in the history of Canon Law. Clergy conferences refer to exclusive meetings of clergymen, convened at the command of the local bishop and conducted under his or at least his delegate's direction and supervision, at designated occasions during the year, for the specific purpose of educating the priests who had the charge and care of souls.

At the very outset, it is apropos to distinguish these ecclesiastical conferences from the solemn and public convocations, which were held by the bishop, the clergy and the faithful in early times. These latter convocations and synods had for their proper purpose the discursive explanation of Christian doctrine and the invention of practical defense against contemporary heresy and false teachings.

Clergy conferences have had various names throughout history, such as consistories, deanery chapters or synods, Kalends, and sessions. In accord with the definition of clergy conferences given above, it is the task of this writer to collect abstractions from the history of this institute as found in papal decrees, in the decrees of plenary and provincial councils, and in the statutes of diocesan synods.

There is evidence of the existence and purpose of clergy conferences as early as the fourth century. The first citation is that Saint Basil of Cappadocia,[1] who died in the year 379, in an official letter to one of his associates named Chilon. Here Saint Basil referred to clerical meetings as an established institute; pointing out their existence, purpose and fruits. His epistle attested to the fact that these conferences were held regularly, but always under the direction of the bishop and that their effects were most edifying. Included among the agenda of the meetings were discussions on the enigmas of the Book of Proverbs, the Apostolic documents, the parables in the Gospels and points of dogmatic and moral theology.

By the sixth century, clergy conferences were constituted as frequent synods; not to be confused with the synods which were legislative in purpose just as the synods of today. For instance, the diocesan synod of Auxerre[2] portrays that the meeting was rather concerned with the practical phases of the priestly ministry, namely discussion of moral and and disciplinary measures.

Weighty authors and commentators[3] state that Saint Charles Borromeo was the founder of clergy conferences. This writer has no intention of minimizing the influence of Saint Charles Borromeo upon this institute but historical evidence points to the fact that clergy conferences were in vogue for centuries befor his day. It is quite true that he initiated a new era in the development of the institute by drawing up definite rules and regulations for conducting the conferences. Thus the present writer maintains that although Saint Charles did much in regard to the institute, he only crystallized what had been customary for centuries. The very important role played by Saint Charles Borromeo will be explored in the third chapter of this historical treatise.

[1] *Epistola XLII* [ad Chilonem], n. 4, in J. P. Migne, *Patrologia Cursus Completus,* Series Graeca (161 vols., Paris, 1857-1866), XXXII, 354 (hereafter cited as *MPG*).

[2] C. 7, L. Bail, *Summa Conciliorum,* (2 vols., Padova, 1723), II, 230.

[3] Berutti, *Institutiones Iuris Canonici* (5 vols., Vol. II, Pars I, Taurini: Marietti, 1943), II, 125; Cocchi, *Commentarium* in Codicem Iuris Canonici (8 vols. in 5, Vol. II, 4. ed., Taurini:Marietti, 1937), II, 110; Wernz-Vidal, *Ius Canonicum* (7 vols. in 8, Vol. II, 3. ed. a R. P. Aguirre, Romae: apud Aedes Universitatis Gregorianae, 1943), Vol. II, *De Personis,* n. 136 (hereafter cited as Wernz-Vidal).

CHAPTER II

THE HISTORY OF THE INSTITUTE BEFORE THE COUNCIL OF TRENT

The diocesan synod, consisting of a single general meeting of the bishop and his clergy, with the specific purpose of discussion, was found to be quite adequate and satisfactory until the rapid expansion of the Church began in the ninth century. The Christian world grew and expanded from territory to territory. The dioceses automatically became larger in population and extent. At times it became impossible, or at least extremely difficult for the local bishop to gather his priests in one place for the general meetings mentioned above. In order to solve this problem, it was decreed that dioceses should be divided into four deaneries, each under a so-called archpriest, and each section was to hold its own meetings.[1] The establishment of the deanery system brought about the necessity of having a definite procedure for conducting the meetings along uniform lines to obtain the desired purpose.[2] Circumstances of the times demanded legislation when the local Bishop could not attend all the conferences personally.

The first document concerning clergy conferences was that of Hincmar, Archbishop of Rheims. In his statutes of the year 852, he referred to the institute as a recognized custom.[3] The meetings convened on the first day of every month and thus the term, " Kalends " was assigned to them. Archbishop Hincmar sought to abolish the absuses which had arisen in conjunction with the actual holding of the conferences. The abuses he condemned in particular were excesses in eating and drinking. It may be

1 Capitulum Herardi, n. 91, in J. P. Migne, *Patrologiae Cursus Completus*, Series Latina (221 vols., Parisiis, 1844-1855), CXXI, 770 (hereafter cited as *MPL*).

2 Thomassinus, *Vetus et Nova Ecclesiae Disciplina* (3 vols., Parisiis: apud Andream Crass, 1787), Tom. I, Pars I, lib. II, cap. V, nn. 1-5.

3 *Concilia Galliae*, Tom. III, in *MPL*, CXXV, 777.

remarked that this abuse was more likely to occur at that time because the conferences were in session for an entire day. Legislation regarding the meetings seemed always to have included a meal for the participants. Bishop Hincmar stressed that the meal should be a simple one, not an extravagant feast. He also prescribed that the priests return home immediately after the closing of the conference. He went on to draw an analogy between these meetings and the "agape" of the Corinthians at the time of Saint Paul. He quoted the very text of Saint Paul[4] condemning these celebrations because of the abuses in the use of food. The decrees of Archbishop Hincmar were later repeated by Regino of Pruem (899).[5]

In 879 Bishop Riculfe[6] of Soissons in France issued to his clergy a constitution in which he commanded that conferences be held on the first day of each month. In these meetings the priests were to discuss all problems concerning their ministry and to settle administrative difficulties which arose in their care of souls.

In the tenth century, Bishop Atto[7] of Vercelli in Italy, fully aware of the utility and advantages of the conferences from his personal experience, designated the monthly discussions for the clergy of his diocese. A Capitulary of his ordered that the priests discuss points regarding the faith, the administration of the Sacraments, ecclesiastical life and customs including any and all the duties which the priesthood entailed. Delinquents and wrong-doers were reprimanded and publicly corrected at such meetings. Burchard of Worms,[8] who died in 1025, incorporated the legislation of Hincmar and Atto in his decretal collection.

In England, the Council of London, (1237),[9] imposed a strict

4 *I Cor.* XI, 17-22.

5 Cf. *De Ecclesiasticis Disciplinis,* Lib. I, cap. 226, in *MPL,* CXXXII, 34-35.

6 *Concilia Galliae,* Tom. I, p. 533, in *MPL,* CXXXI, 231-232.

7 *Capitulare,* c. XXIX, in *MPL,* CXXXIV, 34-35.

8 *Decretum,* Lib. II, cap. CLXIV, in *MPL,* CXL, 653-654.

9 Mansi, *Sacrorum Conciliorum Nova et Amplissima Collectio* (53 vols. in 60, Paris-Arnhem-Leipzig, 1901-1927), XXII, 458 (hereafter cited as Mansi).

obligation upon the so-called archdeacons to convoke deanery conferences frequently and to preside and conduct them personally. The archdeacons were commanded to instruct other priests in matters including the sacraments of baptism, penance, the Eucharist and matrimony. Likewise, this council prescribed that they should diligently inform the clergy about the proper method of celebrating the Holy Sacrifice of the Mass, its meaning, and the administration of the Sacrament of Baptism.

A Synod of Rouen, which was actually held at Pont-Audemer[10] in 1279, decreed that the deans were to reprimand clerics who were negligent or careless about the wearing of the clerical tonsure and this was to take place at the Kalends. The identical rule was introduced at the Council of Lambeth[11] which was conducted in the year 1261. It is important for us that mention was made by the presiding members of this synod and council concerning the existence of clergy conferences as customory and of frequent occurrence.

It would seem safe to state that the actual practice of convoking clergy conferences as a result of decrees of councils and synods, was very widespread in France by the thirteenth century. Clergy conferences were held in some territories of Germany and England by this time but not as universally. In Italy the institute had been introduced, but it did not hold any position of importance.

In the fourteenth century, the Council of Rouen (1335)[12] took occasion to make reference to an existing practice of conducting Kalends in many deaneries. It was also decreed in this council that the Kalends or conferences were useful opportunities for settling disputes on the question of reserved sins.

In 1342 the Council of London[13] designated that special meetings, which were to be conducted three or four times a week, should include the ironing out of problems and the resolving of questions regarding jurisdiction. The superiors having ordinary

[10] C. 21 Mansi, XXIV, 225.

[11] C. 31 Mansi, XXIV, 1071.

[12] C. 11 Mansi, XXV, 1045-1046.

[13] C. 8 Mansi, XXV, 1163.

jurisdiction were the bishops of the dioceses and their archdeacons. Although these meetings fulfilled the necessary requirements for the classification of them as clergy conferences, their object and purpose seem to point to them as an institute similar to the bishops' meeting held in our country yearly.

Shortly before the Council of Trent the Council of Cologne [14] in the year 1536 exacted that provincial and diocesan statutes were to be officially promulgated at the conferences supervised by the rural deans.

[14] Cc. 19-21 Mansi, XXXII, 1205.

CHAPTER III

IMPORTANT INFLUENCES ON THIS INSTITUTE AFTER THE COUNCIL OF TRENT TO THE EIGHTEENTH CENTURY

The Council of Trent [1] had as one of its main concerns, the spiritual affairs of the Church and in particular a sincere desire to further the efficiency and welfare of the clergy. One of the most significant aims of the Council was legislation to initiate a complete intellectual and moral reformation of the clergy. It is not the aim of this treatise to explore the many decrees which pointed out the necessary requirements in candidates for the priesthood. It suffices here to say that the education of clerics before the reception of the sacrament of orders was likewise revised by Tridentine decrees.

Pointed enactments served to revive the institute of clergy conferences in dioceses where the practice had grown exstinct or infrequent.[2] Also, the impetus was given towards its establishment in places where bishops had not adopted the practice before this time. As a result of the decrees of the Council of Trent, it is safe to say that the institute became a general custom for the clergy in all Christian countries.

Article 1. Impetus Given the Institute by Saint Charles Borromeo

Saint Charles Borromeo may be rightly called the champion of the institute of clergy conferences, for he made them a diocesan institution once again after the legislation of the Council of Trent. His work was done in Italy, but his influence became continental. At the I Council of Milan (1565),[3] he designated

[1] Joseph Pelella, *Canones et Decreta Concilii Tridentini* (editio Neopolitana, 1859), Sessio XXV, *de ref.* cc. 2, 4 and 10.

[2] *Loc. cit.*

[3] Pars II, c. 28 Mansi, XXXIV, 42-43.

that conferences be held monthly throughout the entire province. Following the very purpose of the institute and the Council of Trent, he directed that these meetings should have as their aim matters pertaining to pastoral duties and obligations. He went on to specify that the program of the conferences was to include prepared topics and practical discussions on reserved cases, synodal decrees and cases of conscience.

Likewise, he prescribed that each diocese be proportionately divided up into deaneries as we know them today. Every diocese was to have at least five sections or deaneries. The vicar-forane or Rural Dean was to have a definite pre-eminence in each. The dean was instructed to have all members of the clergy in his territory who had the charge of souls meet once each month. He was also to confer with them on points of pastoral administration, cases of conscience, reserved sins and constitutions of previous councils and synods. He was likewise responsible to give an exact account of the proceedings of the meetings to the local bishop.

In the II Council of Milan (1569),[4] Saint Charles took advantage of a second opportunity to foster the spirit of the conferences and the love of scholastic learning so necessary in the life of the ministers of Christ. Every community, if consisting of at least five priests, were to hold a conference once a week. This meeting was to be modeled after the traditional conferences, i.e., a reading was taken from the Catechism of the Council of Trent, cases of conscience were discussed, and consideration was given also to the synodical constitutions. This legislation was primarily constituted for the benefit of the regulars and of the junior clergy.[5]

In 1576, in the IV Council of Milan, it was decreed that the conferences were to be dispensed with during the months of December and January because of the difficulties entailed in travelling and in view of the shortness of the winter days. However, these omissions were to be supplied in the other months.[6]

[4] Decretum XVIII Mansi, XXXIV, 116-117.

[5] *Loc. cit.*

[6] Pars II, c. 15 Mansi XXXIV, 274-275.

This council saw fit to approve and recommend the book, "Instructiones Congregationum Dioecesarum." This compilation of Saint Charles was to be printed and distributed to each priest attending the conference.[7] This book included all the decrees enacted by previous councils and synods regarding clergy conferences.

Little more than a decade after the revival of the conferences, the Sacred Congregation of Bishops and Regulars was questioned as to whether or not those who were not yet ordained were bound to participate in the meetings.[8] The Congregation basing its decision upon the fact that the conferences were designated for the greater honor and glory of God through the priestly ministry, maintained that a bishop was permitted to refuse ordination to one who did not attend the conferences. It will be seen that the same question concerning those who were bound to attend the meetings arose frequently in subsequent years.

The pattern or schedule of a typical conference at this time may be formulated as follows: a) the meeting was either designated to take place on a definite day or simply announced beforehand; b) attendance was compulsory, but no one was admitted except clerics; c) the participants went to confession the evening before; d) Matins were recited in common; e) a solemn procession was led around the Church before the opening of the conference; f) a simple luncheon was served at mid-day; g) appropriate reading concerning the spiritual life and ministry was listened to; h) cases of conscience, which had been previously assigned, were solved; i) devotions in honor of the Blessed Sacrament were assisted at and then the conference was adjourned. All were to return to their respective posts without unnecessary delay.

The Diocese of Aix in France in 1585 established the deanery system with the vicars-forane as superiors. Monthly conferences were prescribed and all points of interest concerning the priestly

[7] *Ibid.*, col. 275.

[8] S. C. Ep. et Reg., *Lucana,* 1 iul. 1579 *Codicis Iuris Canonici Fontes,* cura Emī Petri Card. Gasparri editi (9 vols., Romae: 1923-1939; Vols. VII, VIII, IX editi cura et studio Emī Justiniani Card. Serédi), n. 1351 (hereafter cited as *Fontes*).

ministry were treated at length under the supervision of the deans.[9] The Diocese of Toulouse in France, in 1950, also adopted the decrees of the IV Council of Milan (1576). Two conferences were to be held each week for the junior clergy under strict obligation to attend. Regulars were to be invited to participate.[10]

The Sacred Congregation of Bishops and Regulars received an inquiry in the year 1593 from the diocese of Ferrara, Italy, concerning the perennial question as to those obliged to attend the conferences. Regulars with the charge of souls evidently refused to attend on the claim of exemption. The Congregation declared that all regulars engaged in the ministry of souls were obliged to attend each meeting and refusal to participate could be punished. Suspension was named as a penalty for non-attendance. If they celebrated Holy Mass after being so penalized and not yet absolved, they incurred the further penalty, namely irregularity.[11] The Congregation was approached on the same subject in 1594 by the diocese of Colle di Val d'Elsa in Italy. The reply of the Congregation was as follows: all secular priests were bound to attend, if they had the faculty to hear confessions, but if they were without this faculty, they were only to be urged and exhorted to attend. The final judgment as to the obligation of attendance was left to the prudent enforcement by the bishop.[12]

In 1596, the Diocese of Aquila in Italy took up the idea of Saint Charles Borromeo concerning the conducting of clergy conferences. The deanery system was set up with conferences on cases of conscience in each.[13]

The problem regarding the attendance of regulars at the clergy conferences arose again in the year 1598. The Bishop of Padua in Italy asked the Sacred Congregation of Bishops and Regulars for a clarification of the matter. The response of the

9 Mansi, XXXIV, 1003-1004.

10 Cap. VI Mansi, XXXIV, 1281-1282.

11 S. C. Ep. et Reg., *Ferrarien.*, 13 oct. 1593—*Fontes*, n. 1495.

12 S. C. Ep. et Reg., *Collen.*, 2 aug. 1594—*Fontes*, n. 1515.

13 Mansi XXXIV, 1417-1419.

Congregation carried words of praise for the deanery-system of holding conferences and called attention to the edifying fruits of the meetings. The local bishop was to inform the superiors of regulars that they were to attend the conferences with their subjects under pain of censure and other proportionate penalties.[14]

In 1603, the Diocese of Brixen in the Tyrol was pointed out as having an exemplary arrangement of conducting clergy conferences.[15] The statutes of this diocese gave evidence of the bishop's practical legislation to reform clerical discipline and to repair the inroads of heresy. The schedule of conferences consisted of the following points: a) the announcement of the date beforehand; b) each participant was to celebrate Holy Mass in the presence of the archpriest; c) each one was to give an accurate account of all the details of his personal spiritual life and ministry including a report on the spiritual status of his parish. If his actions were delinquent or if he was guilty of negligence, he could be punished by means of fines or incarceration for a designated time. The proceeds of the fines were to be added to the common fund for the purchase of books or for the Church or were to be given to the poor. The Vicar-General was to check and review all sentences and rely upon his own prudence in enforcing the punishments.

In 1605, the Synod of Chur in Switzerland,[16] ordered that chapters were to be conducted once a month in country districts. Three cases of conscience were presented for discussion at each session and each priest had to submit a written solution of the proposed problems. Priests were also to be examined concerning their spiritual life and doctrine and they were to be questioned on these matters.

Weekly conferences were established by the Synod of Cosenza [17] in Italy (1606), and the next year the I Diocesan Synod

[14] S. C. Ep. et Reg., *Patavina,* 27 maii 1598—*Fontes,* n. 1572.

[15] *Concilia Germaniae,* VIII, 560-561; E. Vacant-E. Mangenot, *Dictionnaire de Théologie Catholique* (15 vols. in 30 and Index, Paris, 1903), III, col. 819 (hereafter cited as *DTC*).

[16] *Concilia Germaniae,* VIII, 641-644, in *DTC,* III, col. 820.

[17] *DTC,* III, col. 820.

of Ravenna,[18] Italy, decreed a weekly conference to be held at the residence of the bishop. In 1607 the Council of Malines ruled that the bishop should convene one conference a year on a day designated by himself.[19]

In 1609 the Cardinal Archbishop of Bordeaux in France established the deanery system in his archdiocese. Monthly conferences were to be conducted under the vicars-forane.[20] This Archbishop was Francis de Sourdis. He was succeeded by his brother Henry in 1628, who in 1632 and 1638, repeated the recommendations of conducting deanery meetings.[21] The archbishop of Lyons in 1627 imposed an obligation upon his clergy to assist at ecclesiastical conferences, and his successors often reiterated the precept. The meetings referred to were held in accord with the ideas laid down by Saint Charles Borromeo.[22]

The Bishop of Fossombrone appealed to the Sacred Congregation of the Council in the year 1650 regarding the problem caused by the non-attendance of regulars at the clergy conferences.[23] The Congregation replied that the bishop should compel all priests, even regulars if charged with the care of souls, to attend the conferences. All other members of the clergy were to be encouraged to assist, but no compulsion was to be employed on them.

In 1720 the Diocese of Trier in the Rhineland instituted monthly conferences under the title of "Congregation of Saint Charles Borromeo." The conferences were to be held with a solemn religious ceremony.[24]

In general, the Bishops of northern Europe strove very earnestly to observe the decrees of the Council of Trent designated for the purpose of reforming the clergy and ecclesiastical

18 Loc. cit.

19 Tit. 7, no. 10, 14, in Thomassinus, *Vetus et Nova Ecclesiae Disciplina*, Pars I, Lib. II, cap. 76, n. III.

20 *DTC*, III, col. 820.

21 *Loc. cit.*

22 *DTC*, III, col. 821.

23 S. C. C., *Forosempronien.*, 3 sept. 1650—*Fontes*, n. 2710.

24 *Concilia Germaniae*, X, 412-417; *DTC*, III, col. 821.

discipline. Provincial and Diocesan Statutes were promulgated and enforced by means of Clergy Conferences modeled after the example set up by Saint Charles Borromeo.[25]

Article 2. The Tuesday Conferences of Saint Vincent de Paul

The efforts of Saint Charles Borromeo and of Saint Vincent de Paul signalize great milestones in the historical development of clergy conferences before the legislation of the present Code of Canon Law. Consideration will now be given to the importance of the Tuesday Conferences of Saint Vincent de Paul.

July 19, 1633, was a very important date. It was the day on which Saint Vincent de Paul called to order the first Tuesday Conference at St. Lazare in Paris.[26] It consisted of a group of secular priests, bound together voluntarily out of the love of God and for the spiritual efficiency of their priestly ministry. At first glance it could appear that this group was made up of religious, especially since they were to live according to a common rule. However, closer scrutiny reveals the fact that they had no intention of embracing the statute of religious in the strict sense of the word. This is brought out by the exact nature, organization and the results of this congregation of secular priests.

Examination of the Tuesday Conferences points to the fact that they were clergy conferences properly so-called, for they fulfilled the conditions of the institute as stated in the first chapter of this treatise. There are two points on which one might raise some question regarding the presence of the conditions necessary for clergy conferences; a) all clergy conferences in the proper sense of the term were to be supervised by the bishop and directed by him, but the Tuesday Conferences were not so convened, and b) all clergy conferences were concerned with the education of the clergy, whereas the Tuesday Conferences were concerned primarily with the sanctification of the attending members. Although the Tuesday Conferences were

[25] *Ibidem*, col. 823.

[26] Pierre Coste, *The Life and Works of Saint Vincent de Paul*, (translated by Joseph Leonard) 3 vols., Westminster, Md.; Newman Press, 1952, II, Chapters 4 and 5.

not the result of episcopal planning, yet they were held with the approval of the bishop. The condition looking to the education of the members was also fulfilled. It is true that the emphasis was shifted from a discussion of doctrines and morals to a more theoretical study of the priestly virtues and the spiritual life, but such a study necessarily touched on the basic principles of doctrines and morals essential in the life of priests.

Saint Vincent de Paul began his work for his fellow-priests in a very prudent manner. At first he was content with determining just the essential features of institution by setting up rules which could be readily adapted and modified in the course of time by practicality and experience before a definite plan was formulated. The members consisted of priests, deacons and subdeacons. Invitation for attendance was preceded by a rigorous investigation. Soon the membership in these conferences became a great honor and a much sought-after privilege. Great scholars among the bishops and parish priests were enrolled; there were over forty doctors from the Sorbonne and twenty-two bishops in the proud ranks.[27]

Once an applicant was admitted, he was bound to follow a strict way of life, which rivalled that of many religious orders. Each member was to make his confession once a week, to participate in the weekly conference, to make regular retreats, to perform special charitable duties assigned to him, to teach catechism to his people, and to do all that he possibly could to promote the spiritual life among fellow-members of the clergy.[28]

The officials of the organization consisted of a director, a prefect with his two assistants, and a secretary. The director, a distinguished member of the congregation, was to supervise each meeting, to hear the opinions of the members, and to give summaries of the discussions. The prefect and his two assistants, who were chosen from the ordinary ranks of the participants, presented the proposals of the members to the director, advised him especially regarding the performance of the practical charitable duties, and also provided for the needs of sick members.

[27] Coste, *op. cit.*, Vol. III, Chapters 4 and 5.

[28] *Loc. cit.*

The secretary drew up records of the minutes of the meetings and attended to correspondence. At the quarterly meetings of these officers in a body, general policies were discussed and duties assigned to the particular members.

Any member who was absent from even one discussion, regardless of the underlying reason, was to submit a written explanation for his absence, or to explain it at the next meeting. Moreover, the participants were always bound to explain in a written report what their opinions were on the matter in hand.

The aim of each meeting was the sincere cultivation of a love and a practice of the priestly virtues through a treatment of the motives that could inspire the putting of the virtues into practice. The conferences sought to point out to their members a general pattern of priestly virtues and the ideals that were suited for the perfecting of their personal lives. The fruits of these meetings were amazing and edifying. Priest-members were not only inflamed in their work with a zeal for souls, but they also were fired with a desire to serve the poor and the uneducated in rural areas. Whenever it proved possible, they took over entire country districts and gave what we call today extensive parish-missions. Another outstanding accomplishment of the institution was indicated in the fact that many of the members were later selected for the episcopacy.[29]

The movement spread with great rapidity. When members were elected bishops, they adopted the practice in their respective dioceses. Among these were the following: Bishop Godeau of Grasse, Bishop Fouquet of Bayonne, Bishop Pavillon of Alet, Bishop Barreau of Carlat, Bishop Vialart of Châlons and Bishop Henry de Maupas du Tour of Puy.[30]

The flourishing system of conferences was abruptly terminated temporarily in 1792 when the French Revolution caused the destruction of all Catholic institutions and when members of the clergy were sought out for persecution with the most vicious in-

[29] *Loc. cit.*

[30] Pierre Coste (translated by Joseph Leonard), *The Life and Labours of Saint Vincent de Paul* (3 vols., London: Burns, Oates and Washbourne, Ltd., 1934-1935), II, 118-149.

tent. However, when the political horizons cleared, associations began to multiply with the same vitality as before.[31]

In 1673 the Archbishop of Paris enacted regulations concerning the previously mentioned system of monthly conferences; which continued to expand in many dioceses. Among his decrees was included one which ordered vicars-forane to supervise discussions or the methods of mental prayer, on the examination of conscience and on the spiritual life in general. He also commanded the establishment of a uniform system for moral direction, and this was to be drawn up and promulgated at the meetings. He likewise endowed the conferences with special indulgences for the faithful who approached the sacraments on the days the meetings were held.[32] The diocese of Amiens in the year 1662, and the diocese of Luçon in the year 1670, aodpted similar rules.[33] In fact, most of the diocesan synods in the latter half of the seventeenth century recommended the conferences very strongly.

The number of meetings varied from diocese to diocese, ranging from two to twelve a year. In general, the average was six a year. The matter of attendance seems to have been quite well determined by this time. However, two inquiries were received by the Sacred Congregation of the Council and one by the Sacred Congregation of Bishops and Regulars on this matter. The two sent to the Congregation of the Council referred to the attendance of the canon penitentiary and the canon jubilarian at the conferences. The decision was that the former was held excused[34] and that the latter could be excused for certain reasons, unless particular statutes and custom demanded the contrary.[35]

The letter to the Sacred Congregation of Bishops and Regulars contained a question about the attendance of priests religious if they were confessors who undertook no other actual work in the care of souls. The answer was that they should be

[31] *Loc. cit.*

[32] *DTC,* III, col. 821.

[33] *Loc. cit.*

[34] S. C. C., 3 oct. 1671—*Fontes,* n. 2822.

[35] S. C. C., 15 mart. 1692—*Fontes,* n. 2927.

exhorted to attend the conferences, but could not be compelled to do so.[36]

Before closing the study of clergy conferences prior to the eighteenth century, one should call attention to the legislation that was enacted in the archdioceses of Benevento and Paris. In 1693 the Provincial Council of Benevento prescribed weekly conferences on cases of conscience and on matter relating to the Church's liturgy.[37] Archbishop Louis Antoine of Paris likewise decreed weekly conferences in 1697.[38] The regulations set down by the Provincial Council of Benevento were very detailed; they were later adopted by the Council of Rome in 1725 with certain appropriate modifications.[39]

[36] S. C. Ep. et Reg., decr., 15 ian. 1682—*Fontes*, n. 1811.

[37] *Acta et Decreta Sacrorum Conciliorum Recentiorum, Collectio Lacensis* (7 vols., Firburgi Brisgoviae: Herder, 1870-1892, Vol. I, cols. 42-43, and 103 (hereafter cited as *Coll. Lac.*).

[38] *Actes de l'eglise de Paris*, I, p. 187, in *DTC*, III, col. 823.

[39] Tit. XVII in *Coll. Lac.*, Vol. I, cols. 435-438.

CHAPTER IV

HISTORY OF CLERGY CONFERENCES FROM THE COUNCIL OF ROME (1725) TO THE PRESENT

As is clear from the preceding pages, clergy conferences had become very widespread throughout the whole of Europe by the beginning of the eighteenth century. Bishops supported the practice and unanimously voiced their praise and approval of the meetings. The Council of Venice joined the long list in 1700 by making the conferences a diocesan institution.[1]

In 1716 an inquiry was sent to the Sacred Congregation of Bishops and Regulars; it concerned the problem of who was bound to attend the conferences. It was asked whether priests who were not confessors could be compelled by fines, censures and other penalties to participate in the meetings. The Congregation decided that such priests could only be urged and exhorted to attend, apart from all compulsion or punishment.[2]

Article 1. The Council of Rome and Other Legislation Prior to the Twentieth Century

Pope Benedict XIII convened a Council of Rome in the year 1725. In it he ordered all the bishops of Europe either to establish or to promote the system of the conferences in their dioceses, if they had not already done so. Pope Benedict XIII saw the inherent value of the meetings and ordered the bishops to keep a personal watch over them. It was his firm conviction that conferences should be held on a weekly basis, and that cases of conscience, alternating between problems of moral theology and liturgy should be discussed at length. He patterned his legislation on that enacted for the Province of Benevento, mention of which has already been made.[3] In the same year, conscious of the need of restoring ecclesiastical discipline in Spain, Pope Bene-

[1] Pars II, cap. XI, in *Col. Lac.*, VI, cols. 306-307.

[2] S. C. Ep. et Reg., *Castri Maris*, 8 maii, 1716—*Fontes*, n. 1832.

[3] Tit. XV, cap. IX, no. XVII, in *Coll. Lac.*, I, cols. 371, 435-438.

dict XIII issued a constitution to the bishops of that country to bind all clerics and beneficiaries to attend conferences concerning cases of conscience and discussions on the Church's liturgy.[4] In an instruction to the Sacred Congregation of the Council, he again portrayed his views on the subject. He instructed the Congregation to investigate whether the conferences on moral cases were being carried out in each diocese, how often they were being held, and who in particular was participating in them.[5] His successor, Pope Clement XII, recommended the conferences very highly in a letter issued from the Sacred Congregation of the Council.[6]

Three pastoral letters on clergy conferences were published by Archbishop Lambertini of Bologna, who later became Pope Benedict XIV. He reviewed the decrees of his predecessors and his own decrees of the year 1731. Later he modified and completed these rules and promulgated them as diocesan law. He decided that the number of meetings should be set at seven each year.[7] When he was elected Pope (Benedict XIV), he issued a constitution on the subject in question. In it he stated that bishops had the right and the duty to question all pastors, even regulars, on the occasion of their parish visitations, concerning their attendance at the conferences.[8]

In the year 1717 the Provincial Council of Tarragona in Spain prescribed that under penalty of fine all pastors and confessors attend the meetings, and that all other priests and clerics not yet ordained should be exhorted to attend. The conferences in Spain were especially concerned with the practical problems of moral theology, the rubrics of the breviary, and the ceremonies of the Mass.[9] The Provincial Council of Avignon in France (1725) called for the holding of monthly conferences on cases of con-

[4] Fontes, n. 283. Also *In supremo,* in Angelus Lucidi, *De Visitatione Sacrorum Liminum,* 3. ed., a Josepho Schneider, 3 vols., Romae, 1883, III, 491.

[5] *DTC,* III, col. 823.

[6] *Loc. cit.*

[7] *Loc. cit.*

[8] Benedictus XIV, const. *Firmandis,* 6 nov. 1744—*Fontes,* n. 349.

[9] Decretum IX, in *Coll. Lac.,* I, col. 762.

science.[10] In the following year the Archbishop of Fermo in Italy insisted that frequent meetings be held, but did not determine any definite number.[11]

In the year 1727 the Diocese of Evreux in France instituted the practice of monthly conferences throughout the year, except during the winter months. The meetings were to be concerned with a study of the Sacred Scriptures and moral theology.[12] The Synods of Sarlat and Mende (both in France) ordered an observance of this system according to the same lines.[13] The Synod of Mount Lebanon (1736) commanded that the conferences be introduced for the study of the Sacred Scriptures and for the discussion of cases of conscience in every monastery.[14] The constitutions of the Synod of Chelmno (Kulm) in Poland in the year 1745, and of the Synod of Ypres, Belgium, in the year 1768, revived the meetings which were to deal with the discussions and solutions of cases of conscience.[15] The Archbishop of Albi in France also reintroduced and incorporated the conferences in his decrees of 1753 and 1763 by means of Synods.[16] Two years later the Archbishop of Boulogne in France initiated the conferences in his diocese.[17]

The first record of the suppression of the conferences was in the year 1763. Bishop Brouas of Toul in France abolished the meetings because, as he claimed, the members of the cleregy used them as an opportunity to criticize episcopal administration in his diocese.[18] The first bishops of Nancy and Saint-Die (both in France) refused to introduce the conferences in their respective dioceses.[19]

[10] Tit. XXXVII, cap. XIII, in *Coll. Lac.*, I, col. 558.

[11] Tit. VIII, in *Coll. Lac.*, I, col. 598.

[12] No. XII, in *Coll. Lac.*, I, col. 626.

[13] Cap. II, no. 7, in *Coll. Lac.*, II, col. 104.

[14] *DTC*, III, col. 824.

[15] *Concilia Germaniae*, X, 521-523 in *DTC*, III, col. 824.

[16] *Concilia Germaniae*, X, 666 in *DTC*, III, col. 824.

[17] *Loc. cit.*

[18] *Loc. cit.*

[19] *Loc. cit.*

In 1769 the Bishop of Saint Malo in France praised and recommended the conferences very strongly.[20] Between the years 1776 and 1782 the Archbishop of Trier reorganized the meetings with modifications of the rules designed by Saint Charles Borromeo.[21]

In Italy, the Bishops of Senigallia (Sinigaglia) (1737), of Fano (1731), of Viterbo (1733), of Foligno (1763) and also the Abbot of Farfa called for the holding of meetings concerning cases of conscience.[22]

In the year 1700 it was decreed that the conferences should be held in Canada, but it was not until 1743 that the order was carried out by the clergy.[23]

Because of the ravages of the French Revolution, the nineteenth century was a period of restoration and revival also in regard to clergy conferences. At the turn of the century progress can be detected only in countries other than France. In 1801 the Archbishop of Fribourg, Switzerland, and in 1811 the Bishop of Mainz in Germany, restored the system of meetings in their diocese in accord with the pattern of the previous century.[24] The diocese of Anagni in Italy resumed the conferences on cases of conscience in the year 1805.[25] The Provincial Council of Tuam in Ireland, convened in 1817, established monthly meetings from April to October.[26]

In 1820, the diocese of Metz in France was the first of that country to reintroduce the conferences. Others that followed were: Valence (1823), Lyons (1824), San-Brieuc (1825), Coutances (1828), Nancy (1830), Autun (1932), Saint Die (1833), Avignon (1840), Perigueux (1837), Meaux (1838), Alençon (1840) and Paris (1841).[27] The Bishops of Mende and Verdun

20 *Loc. cit.*

21 *Loc. cit.*

22 *Loc. cit.*

23 *Loc. cit.*

24 *Loc. cit.*

25 *Loc. cit.*

26 Decretum I, in *Coll. Lac.*, III, col. 761.

27 *DTC*, III, col. 824.

tried to reintroduce the meetings, but at first were unsuccessful. It was only at a later date that they were able to do so.[28]

In reviewing this new growth of clergy conferences, a brief conspectus of the development in the individual countries is in order.

In Belgium the Archbishop of Malines established two separate systems of conferences in the year 1836. One group was made up of pastors alone, the other, of assistants. In 1851 the Bishop of Liége designated monthly conferences for the clergy living in the city, and bi-monthly conferences for the clergy in the rural areas.[29] The diocese of Bruges organized the conferences in 1854 on a monthly basis with a special annual report to be presented to the Bishop.[30] In the diocese of Namur the priests themselves took the initiative to set up the conferences. Subsequently in 1866, the bishop officially established the meetings.[31] It is very interesting to note that it was in Belgium that a program of conferences on social problems was introduced for the first time in the history of the institute. It is true that certain dioceses in Italy included particular social problems in the discussions, v.g., the care of the poor, but such points were only part of the agenda.[32]

In Ireland the Plenary Council of Thurles, convened in 1850, determined the number of meetings at four times a year as a minimum.[33] The III Provincial Council of Tuam in 1858 increased the number to at least six conferences each year. This council also indicated that the subject matter for these meetings should encompass cases of conscience and the rubrics of the Mass.[34]

After the re-establishment of the hierarchy in England, the I Provincial Council of Westminster in the year 1852 drew up defi-

28 *Loc. cit.*

29 *Ibidem,* col. 825.

30 *Loc. cit.*

31 *Loc. cit.*

32 *Loc. cit.*

33 Chapter XVII, no. 22, in *Coll. Lac.*, III, col. 786.

34 Cap. VII, no. 2, in *Coll. Lac.*, III, col. 876.

nite rules for clergy conferences. The meetings were to include theological and liturgical matters on their agenda. Under this proposed system, much was left to the discretion of the bishop—he set the number, method and subjects of the discussions. However, the council did make uniform rules with reference to the presiding officer and the clergy in attendance, and it likewise prescribed that each participant was to write out his solutions to the proposed problems.[35] The diocesan Synod of Liverpool, in the year 1853, designated the number of the conferences to be at least six during the year. Again it was demanded that written solutions were to be furnished by all the attending clergy for the cases under discussion.[36]

The I Council of the English, Dutch and Danish Colonies, held in the year 1854, set up the conferences on cases of conscience and questions of the liturgy.[37] These same colonies in the II Council, held in the year 1867, decided that each bishop was to arrange a practical system of meetings as local conditions warranted.[38] In the year 1844, the I Provincial Council of Australia legislated that conferences be held in each deanery at a minimum of three times a year.[39]

The Provincial Council of Utrecht, in the year 1865, gave official recommendation and recognition for the meetings, and advised that the institution be promoted and encouraged by every possible means.[40]

In the Germanic countries the conferences spread with edifying rapidity. The Bishop of Augsburg in the year 1829 established and promoted the clergy meetings in his diocese. His beginning gave the great impetus to the system in and throughout Germany.[41] In the year 1832 the Bishop of Trier set the number of the meetings at six for the year and designated that the

[35] Decret. XXIV, no. 8, in *Coll. Lac.*, III, col. 940.

[36] *DTC*, III, col. 825.

[37] Sectio II, no. 4, in *Coll. Lac.*, III, col. 1100.

[38] Stat. VI, *Coll. Lac.*, III, col. 1045.

[39] Tit. IX, cap. III, *Coll. Lac.*, V, col. 918.

[40] Tit. X, cap. III, *Coll. Lac.*, V, col. 918.

[41] *DTC*, III, col. 825.

matter for discussion should relate to problems in all of the theological sciences, including asceticism.[42] The Provincial Council of Cologne, conducted in the year 1860, praised the utility and advantages of the conferences, prescribing them for the entire province.[43]

In the year 1856, Pope Pius IX issued to the bishops of Austria a letter in which he incorporated his personal recommendations relative to the conferences and indicated the material that called for discussion. He praised the system and insisted that meetings should be held in every section of each diocese. Thus there could readily be promoted the zeal for sacred knowledge among the clergy. Matters of theology and liturgy along with the factors touching the disciplinary rules of the sacred rites were to make up the program. One of the priests was to be assigned for the delivery of a sermon on priestly duties.[44] Likewise, every priest was bound to participate in the meetings.

The Provincial Councils of Vienna in 1858,[45] of Esztergom (Gron) in 1858,[46] of Colocza (Hungary) in 1863,[47] and of Prague in Bohemia in the year 1860, took up the Pope's plan, so that the system of clergy conferences became uniform and widespread in the Austro-Hungarian Empire.[48]

The movement flourished throughout Italy under the auspices of the Holy See in accord with the pattern outline by Saint Charles Borromeo, i.e., discussions on matters of the liturgy, on cases of conscience and on moral obligations. The meetings were held twice a month. In 1849, the bishops of Umbria, Italy, established the conferences for the discussing of matters of moral theology in their dioceses.[49] The next year the bishop of Loreto instituted monthly conferences in a synodal constitution.[50] The

[42] *Loc. cit.*

[43] Tit. III, cap. XXXVI, in *Coll. Lac.*, V, col. 379.

[44] *Coll. Lac.*, V, col. 1246.

[45] Tit. VI, no. 3, *Coll. Lac.*, V, col. 58.

[46] Tit. VI, Cap. VI, *Coll. Lac.* V, cols. 207-208.

[47] *Loc. cit.*

[48] Tit. IV, Cap. VI, in *Coll. Lac.*, VI, Col. 756.

[49] Tit. VIII, no. II, in *Coll. Lac.*, VI, col. 756.

[50] Sect. VI, no. XXVIII, in *Coll. Lac.*, VI, cols. 786-787.

bishops of Sicily ordered the meetings to be conducted at least once every two months.[51] The Provincial Council of Venice, in the year 1856, extended the program of the conferences to include the study of the Sacred Scriptures, of dogmatic and moral theology, and of the liturgy.[52] The diocese of Urbino followed the example of the bishop of Loreto and imposed the obligation of monthly conferences, consonant with the prescriptions of the Council of Rome (1725).[53] In the year 1892 the archbishop of Benevento, through a synod, prescribed that there should be at least ten conferences each year, with all the members of the clergy in attendance and with all the participants presenting written solutions for the cases under discussion.[54] Because of civil upheavals it was very difficult for the clergy on the coast of Spain and Portugal to gather for the conferences. In fact, exclusive meetings of the clergy were frowned upon and suspect. It would have been perilous and dangerous to arouse the civil authorities by closed meetings of the priests. As an inevitable result, the practice gradually became extinct.[55]

In the United States, where the growth of the Church was almost miraculous, the progress of the institute was rapid in the nineteenth century. In 1855 the I Provincial Council of Cincinnati prescribed that the conferences should be conducted in accord with the local conditions, but as often as feasible.[56] The II Provincial Council of Saint Louis, convoked in 1858, decreed that bishops should preside over all the conferences held in their territories.[57] The II and III Provincial Councils of Cincinnati (1858 and 1861 respectively) issued to the clergy a pastoral letter that insisted upon a faithful attendance at the conferences.[58] The II Plenary Council of Baltimore (1866) regulated the fre-

[51] Tit. II, cap. II, no. 6-7, in *Coll. Lac.*, VI, col. 817.

[52] Pars II, cap. XVIII, in *Coll. Lac.*, VI, col. 318.

[53] Pars II, tit. VIII, no. CLXIII, in *Coll. Lac.*, cols. 54-55, 100-102.

[54] *DTC,* III, col. 826.

[55] *Loc. cit.*

[56] Decretum V, in *Coll. Lac.*, III, col. 195.

[57] *Loc. cit.*

[58] Decreta III et XII, in *Coll. Lac.*, III, col. 420.

quency of the conferences and prescribed a minimum of two to four during the year.[59] The X Provincial Council of Baltimore (1869) left it to the judgment of the bishops whether the conferences should be held once every three months.[60] The VIII Diocesan Synod of Baltimore (1875) designated definite rules for the conduct of the meetings in the archdiocese.[61]

In Canada, the I Provincial Council of Quebec, in the year 1851, recommended written solutions for practical cases on the part of the members attending the conferences.[62] Two years later the Archbishop of Québec determined the number at four each year, and formulated a definite program for the meetings.[63] In the year 1854 the II Provincial Council of Québec stressed the moral advantages to be gained from regular participation in the conferences.[64] The I Provincial Council of Halifax in the year of 1857, obligated priests, under penalty of suspension, to attend four conferences each year.[65]

Latin America took its place in this matter among the other countries in the Western Hemisphere. The Provincial Council of Mexico in 1849 recommended that bishops should promote the conferences in their dioceses.[66] The I Council of Quito (Ecuador), conducted in 1863, imposed obligatory attendance at the meetings.[67] The I Provincial Council of Brazil, held in New Grenada five years later, established the conferences throughout the province.[68] The Plenary Council of Latin America, convened in Rome in the year 1899, ordered the restoration and strongly encouraged the continuance of regular

[59] Cap. IV, no. 68, in *Coll. Lac.*, III, col. 420.

[60] Congregatio Secunda Privata—*Coll. Lac.*, III, cols. 584-585.

[61] *Synodus Dioecesana Baltimorensis Octava* (Baltimore: John Murphy and Sons, 1876), pp. 24-26.

[62] Decretum XIII, no. 9, in *Coll. Lac.*, III, col. 615.

[63] *DTC*, III, col. 826.

[64] Decret. XIV, no. 9, in *Coll. Lac.*, III, col. 650.

[65] Decret. XVIII, no. 18, in *Coll. Lac.*, III, col. 753.

[66] Sess. III, no. 6, in *Coll. Lac.*, VI, col. 713.

[67] Decret. IV, no. 9, *Coll. Lac.*, VI, cols. 403-404.

[68] Tit. VIII, cap. III, in *Coll. Lac.*, VI, col. 553.

conferences, leaving definite details to the discretion of the individual bishops.[69]

The Council of Smyrna ordered monthly meetings in 1869.[70] Also in the same year the Congregation for the Propagation of the Faith sent to the Vicars-apostolic of India a letter that ordered the system of conferences. The main concern of the meetings was a program of studies of the ecclesiastical sciences.[71]

Article 2. Present-Day Legislation Concerning Clergy Conferences

The legislation of the Code of Canon Law, as it stands today in canon 131, resulted, in part at least, from the petitions presented by the bishops of France and Germany. These bishops had requested, already in the previous century, that a universal law be enacted which would bind all the bishops of the world in the matter of clergy conferences. The French bishops [72] sought that such meetings be conducted in all the dioceses at least six or seven times each year. They prescribed that all priests were to attend the conferences in their respective deaneries or territories, and the discussions were to concern subjects which were consonant with the sacred sciences. The bishops of Germany [73] voiced the same desire relative to the subject-matter of the conferences, but suggested that the meetings be held even more frequently—once every two weeks, or at last on a monthly basis.

Canon 131 of the present Code of Canon Law seems to have formulated a compromise between the petitions offered by the bishops of France and of Germany. No doubt the legislator also had in mind the beneficial results of the conferences, especially for priests in the active ministry of souls, when he established the universal law binding all ordinaries to institute

69 *DTC,* III, col. 828.

70 Sectio III, cap. V, no. 2, in *Coll. Lac.,* VI, col. 574.

71 S. C. de Prop. Fidei, instr. (ad Vic. Ap. Indiar. Orient.), 8 sept. 1869, no. 11, in *Coll. Lac.,* VI, cols. 665-666.

72 Postulata a pluribus Galliae Episcopis Papae Pio IX, 1869, in *Coll Lac.,* VII, col. 834.

73 Postulata complurium Germaniae Episcoponum, 8 ian. 1870, in *Coll. Lac.,* VII, col. 873.

and promote the meetings. The legislator also saw fit to sanction this law with penalties according to the norms given in canon 2377. Secular priests, if they are contumacious, are to be punished with proportionate penalties. It is left to the prudent discretion of the local ordinary to determine just what these penalties should be. The same norm holds for even the exempt priests religious, if they have the care of souls. If the guilty persons are religious with diocesan faculties, the ordinary may suspend them from hearing the confessions of seculars.[74]

There has been one inquiry on the interpretation of the law as stated above concerning clergy conferences. The clause, " Who have the care of souls ", called for clarification. It was asked of the Commission for the Authentic Interpretation of the Code whether priests religious who are catechists, or assistants in parishes, or chaplains dependent upon the pastor in hospitals and other pious houses, were included in the term. The Commission gave its reply in the negative relative to catechists of religious status, and in the affirmative relative to assistants and chaplains, if according to canon 475, § 6, they are taking the place of the pastor and helping him in the entire parochial ministry.[75] This decision of the Commission is entirely in harmony with decisions given in the history of the institute by bishops and by the Roman Congregations concerning the members of the clergy bound to participate in the conferences.

[74] Bouscaren-Ellis, *Canon Law, A Text and Commentary* (2. printing, Milwaukee: The Bruce Publishing Co., 1948), p. 111.

[75] *Acta Apostolicae Sedis, Commentarium Officiale* (Romae 1909-1929; Civitate Vaticana, 1929-), XXVII (1935), 92; see also T. Lincoln Bouscaren, *The Canon Law Digest* (3 vols. and supplements, Milwaukee: Bruce Publishing Co., Vol. I [1934], Vol. II [1943], Vol. III [1954], Supplements for 1953 and 1954 in 1954, for 1955 in 1956), II, 53.

PART II

CANONICAL COMMENTARY

PRELIMINARY REMARKS

As has been set forth in the foreword of the historical part of this work, the present writer restricts the history and commentary on clergy conferences to those priests who receive mention in canon 131. This canon concerns all priests, whether secular or religious, to whose care and direction the faithful of the Catholic Church are entrusted.

The Code of Canon Law summaries its entire legislation on clerical conferences in three canons and invokes the sanction of the law in another. Canon 131 is the first of these in the Code: it deals with the conferences and outlines the fundamental notions of the legislation. It is definitely the basic canon on clergy conferences. The text of the canon is quoted here.

> Can. 131, § 1. In civitate episcopali et in singulis vicariatibus foraneis saepius in anno, diebus arbitrio Ordinarii loci praestituendis, conventus habeantur, quos collationes seu conferentias vocant, de re morali et liturgica; quibus addi possunt aliae exercitationes, quas Ordinarius opportunas iudicaverit ad scientiam et pietatem clericorum promovendam.
>
> § 2. Si conventus haberi difficile sit, resolutae quaestiones scriptae mittantur, secundum normas ab Ordinario statuendas.
>
> § 3. Conventui interesse, aut, deficiente conventu, scriptam casuum solutionem mittere debent, nisi a loci Ordinario exemptionem antea expresse obtinuerint, tum omnes sacerdotes saeculares, tum religiosi licet exempti curam animarum habentes et etiam, si collatio in eorum domibus non habeatur, alii religiosi qui facultatem audiendi confessiones ab Ordinario obtinuerunt.

Canon 131, then, gives us the concept of the conferences, suggests their frequency, outlines the subject-matter, delineates their purpose, and indicates which members of the clergy are bound to attend the meetings.

The other two pertinent canons supplement canon 131 and explicitly refer to it. The penal canon refers to it explicitly. In the first paragraph of canon 448, there are designated the duties of the rural dean (vicar forane) in regard to the conferences. It reads as follows:

> Vicarius foraneus debet, diebus ab Episcopo designatis, convocare presbyteros proprii districtus ad conventus seu collationes de quibus in can. 131 eisdemque praeesse; ubi vero plures habeantur huiusmodi coetus in variis districtus locis, invigilare ut rite celebrentur.

The same conferences are prescribed for all religious in canon 591. It is not however within the scope of this thesis to include a treatment of the conferences of religious, although apropos references to them will be necessary in this treatment.

Canon 2377 is, of course, a penal canon and explicitly refers to canon 131. It is listed with the penalties which invoke a sanction for obligations that attach to the clerical and religious states of life. It reads:

> Sacerdotes contra praescriptum can. 131, § 1 contumaces, Ordinarius pro suo prudenti arbitrio puniat; quod si fuerint religiosi confessarii curam animarum non gerenetes, eos ab audiendis saecularium confessionibus suspendat.

Another canon may be mentioned here. Canon 303 suggests the holding of similar meetings in mission lands. It reads:

> Prout siverit opportunitas, missionarios saltem praecipuos tum religiosos tum saeculares proprii territorii congregent semel saltem in anno, ut possint ex singulorum experientia et consilio deducere quae sint ordinanda perfectius.

This canon, however, does not enact a strict law, since it only suggests an annual meeting of the superiors with the principal missionaries if the opportunity presents itself. Besides, it is known that these conferences differ from the conferences mentioned in canon 131. A letter of the Sacred Congregation for the Propagation of the Faith of the 3rd of December, 1869, lauded these meetings as aiming at a unity of spirit among the missionaries, at a perfection of the sacred ministry, and at the preservation of a uniform discipline.[1]

A careful reading of the canons quoted above clearly reveals that the law itself leaves much that concerns the clergy conferences to a discretionary determination on the part of the ordinary. The power of the bishop in his restricted territory is one of the facets of law in the Church. He is granted this legislative power by canon 335, § 1.[2] This same canon, however, places a restriction upon the legislative power of the bishop by stating that his power is to be used in accordance with the sacred canons. The phrase, *ad normam sacrorum canonum,* must be emphasized. It not only restricts the bishop's power of legislation for his diocese contrary to the actual text of the general law of the Code of Canon Law but also implies that his legislation is to be in accord with the spirit of the law.[3]

In order to elaborate upon the importance of this point, it seems appropriate to quote directly the following passage from Ryan's dissertation on the principles of episcopal jurisdiction. He writes:

> His (the bishop's) legislation *secundum ius* is directed to the adaptation of the higher law to his diocese. The higher law is the superior legislator's mind as to the means of procuring a particular end. In accommodating the higher law to the specific territorial characteristics of his diocese, the bishop must take cognizance of both the mind of the legislator and the purpose which the superior legislator intends, since both of these must be substantially respected and preserved intact.[4]

Likewise, the adaptation of a general law of the Code to the particular needs of a diocese is not a matter independent of the

1 Wernz-Vidal, II, n. 549.

2 Ryan, *Principles of Episcopal Jurisdiction,* The Catholic University of America Canon Law Studies, n. 120 (Washington, D. C.: The Catholic University of America Press, 1939), pp. 79-144.

3 Edward Roelker, *Invalidating Laws* (Paterson, New Jersey: St. Anthony's Guild Press, 1955), pp. 57-59.

4 Ryan, *op. cit.,* p. 133.

Code of Canon Law. The bishop must follow the general outlines of the universal law as far as they are expressly designated in the Code. As to the rest, he can adapt the general law, but he cannot legislate contrary to the explicit provisions and the spirit of the universal law. It is his task to particularize the general law at his discretion for the temporal and spiritual mood of his subjects. The bishop can, then, whenever the universal law admits particularization by permissive laws, make definite regulations which he judges necessary or useful for his diocese.[5]

It must also be kept in mind that the bishop can legislate *praeter ius* in view of specific diocesan needs.[6] Thus any particular legislation which is either *secundum ius* or *praeter ius* can be enacted by ordinaries in their respective diocese. Particular provisions which are *contra ius* cannot stand, unless legitimate custom has done away with the general law.

It seems necessary to keep the preceding principles in mind in exploring the modern commentary on clergy conferences, since much is left to the discretionary measures of the ordinary. Even the penal canon is indeterminate in regard to the possible penalties to be imposed for failure to comply with the obligation of attendance at the conferences.[7]

The present universal legislation on clergy conferences is an outgrowth of previous particular enactments. It has been already stated that the canons dealing with the conferences resulted, in part at least, from the petitions presented to the Holy See by the bishops of France and Germany.[8]

The French bishops suggested that the general law contain a prescription designating that the conferences be conducted at least six or seven times each year. They likewise offered the suggestion that all priests attend the meetings in their respective deaneries or territories, and that the discussions relate to subjects

[5] Roelker, *op. cit.*, p. 61.

[6] Signatura Apostolica, 15 dec. 1923: ". . . Ipsi (episcopi) plena potestate praediti sunt condendi leges ac decreta praeter ius, scilicet, quae iuri communi non adversentur."—*AAS*, XVI (1924), 107.

[7] See canon 2377.

[8] Cf. *supra.*, p. 43.

consonant with the sacred sciences.[9] The bishops of Germany delineated the same subject-matter, but advised that the meetings be held as often as once every two weeks, or at least on a monthly basis.[10]

It seems, at least to the present writer, that the compilers of the Code of Canon Law wisely left the determination of the frequency of the conferences to a great extent to particular legislation. This point will be treated extensively in Chapter VI, with reference to the phrase "*saepius in anno,*" as contained in canon 131.

As has been said, there is one canon which prescribes in a general manner the penalties that can be imposed for non-compliance with the obligation of attending the conferences.[11] This canon is also a reflection of the pre-Code penalties invoked against negligent absence from the meetings.[12] Here again, only the broad outlines of the possible penalties are mentioned. However, in line with the general tenor of penal law in the present legislation, canon 2377 definitely postulates a contumacious refusal of attendance, for only then can the ordinary impose proportionate penalties at his discretion. Since this canon expressly states that, if the guilty person is a religious who, not having the care of souls but enjoying the faculties to hear confessions in the diocese, does not attend the meetings [13] in his own religious house, the ordinary may suspend him from hearing the confessions of seculars. The suspension from hearing the confessions of seculars appears to be the sole and therefore also the maximum penalty for the violation of the obligation of attendance at the conferences on the part of religious who have confessional jurisdiction.

[9] Postulata a pluribus Gall. Ep. Papae Pio IX, 1869—*Coll. Lac.*, VII, col. 834.

[10] Postulata complurium German. Ep., 8 ian. 1870—*Coll. Lac.*, VII, col. 873.

[11] Canon 2377.

[12] Cf. *supra*, pp. 31ff.

[13] Can. 591.

CHAPTER V

THE NOTION, PURPOSE AND SUBJECT-MATTER OF CLERGY CONFERENCES

First of all, it is very necessary to have a clear and concise concept of just what the term clergy conferences includes. Clergy conferences must always be distinguished from diocesan synods, as they are known today. Synods are convoked in a formal manner, are legislative in their tenor, and involve only the principal priests of the diocese.[1] Clergy conferences, on the other hand, are more or less informal meetings of all the priests of the diocese who are engaged in the care of souls for the discussion of matters of moral theology and liturgy. To these matters for discussion the ordinary may add other exercises that he judges suitable to the promotion of knowledge and piety among his clergy.[2]

There is no precise definition of the conferences in the Code of Canon Law. However, from their description in the relevant canons, it is not difficult to ascertain just what is meant by clergy conferences in the present discipline of the Church's universal law.

Article 1. The Notion of Clergy Conferences

Before the promulgation of the new Code of Canon Law, the essence, subject-matter and purpose of the conferences were numerous and varied. It has been seen that the Council of Rome, convened in the year 1725, consolidated to some extent the concept of the conferences.[3] In this council, Pope Benedict XIII brought the conferences under a stricter surveillance of the bishops and designated the material object of the conferences, which was to center upon cases of conscience with alter-

[1] Can. 365, § 1.

[2] Can. 131, § 1.

[3] Cf. *supra*, p. 18.

nating discussions on problems of moral theology and liturgy. As was mentioned before, Pope Benedict XIII patterned his constitution upon that which had been enacted for the Province of Benevento in the year 1693.[4] However, it was not until the general legislation of the Code of Canon Law took effect that the concept of the conferences became a settled matter. The new Code of Canon Law did not with reference to the conferences predetermine a stereotyped pattern. It established only the general outlines of the conferences and left great liberty to the judgment and discretion of the ordinaries regarding the accidentals. The essential elements must now necessarily be the same for the universal Church. The designation of these elements is contained in canon 131. This canon describes clergy conferences as meetings or gatherings of the clergy for a professional discussion of problems relating to moral theology and the liturgy, to which other exercises may be added at the discretion of the ordinary if he considers them conducive to the advancement of learning and to the piety of the clergy.[5]

The history of the institute known as clergy conferences in the sense mentioned above reveals certain elements as relevant factors in these meetings.[6] For instance, the meetings were called Kalends because they were held once a month. At other times, they were appropriately named sessions. Consistories, deanery chapters and synods also played a part in the history of the conferences at different periods. The Code of Canon Law with a similar sense of freedom designates them as conferences or gatherings,[7] as meetings,[8] and as discussion groups for the solution of moral and liturgical problems.[9] The names of the conferences also vary in the councils and diocesan synods held after the promulgation of the new Code of Canon Law.[10] In English,

[4] Tit. XV, cap. IX, no. XVII, in *Coll. Lac.*, I, cols. 371; 435-438.

[5] § 1.

[6] *Supra*, p. 3.

[7] Can. 131, 448.

[8] Canon 448.

[9] Canon 591.

[10] S. Galasso, *De Cleri Collationibus* (Potentiae: Ex Typis Marii Nucei, 1940), p. 95, nota 6.

use is made of such terms as clergy conferences, deanery meetings, or diocesan conferences.

A briefer and less determinate definition of the conferences is given by Coronata when he describes them as meetings of priests for the discussion of determined matters pertaining to the sacred sciences.[11] Coronata fails to make any distinction between the necessary and optional subject-matter of the conferences. The Code of Canon Law determines the matter of moral theology and liturgy as necessary matter of the conferences; other subjects chosen by the bishop when judged by him as conducive to the advancement of learning and the piety of the clergy comprise the optional subject-matter.

A good descriptive definition of the conferences designates them as gatherings or meetings of all priests, especially of those who exercise the care and direction of souls, either in the episcopal city or in a rural deanery, for the definite purpose of informing themselves on matters of moral theology and liturgy and on other duties and obligations pertaining to the pastoral office or to the discipline of clerical life.[12]

Article 2. The Purpose of Clergy Conferences

In the very constitution of the Catholic Church, the clerical state is endowed with special dignity. However, to this dignity there corresponds a proportionately grave responsibility. It is only reasonable, then, that the Church is ever solicitous about the clergy to whose charge the souls of the faithful are entrusted. The legislator, by means of the provisions of Canon Law, points out the ways and means most suitable for the necessary competence and proficiency of the human ministers of Christ.

The purpose or final object of the conferences is not indicated directly or explicity in the sacred canons. Some writers, however, state the contrary. For instance, Zaplotnik asserts that

[11] "Sacerdotum conventus ad disserendum de determinatis materiis ad scientias sacras pertinentibus."—*Institutiones*, I, n. 190.

[12] E. Eichmann—K. Moersdorf, *Lehrbuch des Kirchenrechts*, (6. ed., 3 vols., Paderborn, Schoeningh: 1949-1950), I, n. 44; Wernz-Vidal, II (1943), n. 137, p. 188; Galasso, *De Cleri Collationibus*, pp. 94-97; Augustine, *A Commentary on the New Code of Canon Law* (8 vols., 2, ed., St. Louis and London, 1918-1924), II, 75-77.

the purpose of the conferences is portrayed in the first paragraph of canon 131, wherein it is stated that the meetings be convened for the discussion of matters of moral theology and liturgy, to which the ordinary can add other exercises if he judges them opportune for the furtherance of learning and piety among the clergy.[13] Zaplotnik concludes that the purpose of the conferences is explicitly stated in canon 131, but actually all that is stated in the canon is the norm that the bishop should follow in determining the optional matter of the conferences.

Therefore, the Code of Canon Law does not delineate explicitly the purpose of the meetings, but hints at it only implicitly. The final object of the conferences is not only the preservation but also the promotion or furtherance of knowledge and piety on the part of the clergy. This conclusion is drawn from the fact that the exercises where prescription is left to the discretion of the ordinary are to be such as prove suitable for advancing the learning and piety of the clergy. This likewise attests, though only indirectly and implicitly, that the purpose of the meetings is the furtherance of competency and proficiency on the part of clerics through the mediums of learning and piety.[14]

This idea is even more apparent if the context of canon 131 is carefully considered. This canon can be understood not only as a corollary and a complement for the preceding canons on the obligations of clerics, but also as a pertinent resumé of the listed duties and obligations. Canons 124–128 prescribe the exercises of piety consonant with the life of clerics. Then, in order to forestall neglect of clerical studies, canon 129 orders a continued study of the sacred sciences after ordination or after the completion of the theological studies. Underlying these rules is the principle that knowledge without clerical living makes a priest arrogant, and clerical living without learning renders

13 "Finis conferentiarum divulgatur in can. 131, par. 1, ubi statuuntur tales conventus habendos esse 'de re morali et liturgia [sic], quibus addi possunt aliae exercitationes, quas Ordinarius opportunas judicaverit ad scientiam et pietatem clericorum promovendam'."—Zaplotnik, *De Vicariis Foraneis* (Washington, D. C.: The Catholic University of America, 1927), p. 114.

14 Blat, II, *De Personis,* Pars I, n. 68; Galasso, *De Cleri Collationibus,* p. 109.

him useless. Proficiency in the sacred sciences provides the foundation which directly aids the attainment of the apostolic purpose of the priesthood. Canon 130 demands an examination for three consecutive years after ordination in the various subjects of theology for all priests. In addition, then, as if sensing the insufficiency of these measures, the legislator established further provisions in canon 131 to enhance the intellectual and moral status of Christ's ministers.

Other commentators and writers in their treatment of the purpose of clergy conferences, point to the final object as the perfection of proficiency in the exercise of the pastoral office. Wernz-Vidal do so and point out that the advancement of the learning and the piety of the clergy is only a general or secondary end of the conference.[15] Zaplotnik, writing in the same tenor, stated that the promotion and furtherance of learning and piety are only secondary ends of the conferences.[16]

But if one distinguishes between the immediate and the mediate ends of the conferences, one will find that the immediate final object of the meetings is the preservation and promotion of learning and piety among priests. It is the opinion of the present writer that the advancement of knowledge and piety is the primary and immediate end of the conferences. The other ends, though very important from a practical point of view, are secondary or mediate in relation to the advancement of learning and piety, inasmuch as they result from the immediate end. Therefore, the proficiency of priests in the pastoral office, by way of example, is mediate or secondary, since it follows as an automatic result of knowledge and piety. Besides, in the logical order, it is evident that learning and piety are the foundation

[15] "Ex iure Codicis conferentiae seu collationes sunt conventus cleri, qui praecipue ordinantur ad perficiendam vitam pastoralem sacerdotum, eis iuvamen scientiae praestando in recta administratione sacramenti poenitentiae et observatione sacrorum rituum per resolutionem casuum de re morali et liturgica." *Ius Canonicum,* II, (1943), n. 137.

[16] "Primarius et particularis finis est ut sacerdotes perficiant suam scientiam, praesertim in rite audiendis confessionibus et accurate observandis rubricis sacrorum rituum . . . Finis secundarius et generalis est, ut sacerdotes foveant studium theologicum ad firmandum et amplificandam summam scientiarum sacrarum, et augeant pietatem"—*De Vicariis Foraneis,* p. 114.

of success in the life of priests. Once this bulwark is firmly established, the mediate or secondary ends of the conferences can easily follow. In other words, knowledge and piety are the means which are most apt to effect efficient directors of souls.

The secondary ends of the conferences are not to be overlooked or underestimated. These include a desirable uniformity in the exercise of the direction of souls, the solution of personal and common problems by consultative discussion and counsel, the search for more effective means as an aid for the souls entrusted to their care, and the mutual exchange of advice, courage and consolation in their difficult and important work.

Thus it is quite evident that the purpose of the conferences is concentrated on the preservation and promotion of learning and piety in the present universal legislation. The training received in the seminary affords a good foundation, but there is still much to be acquired, especially by actual experience with the problems of souls. Besides, the knowledge obtained in the seminary may soon disappear apart from its continual application by way of personal study and group discussion.

Article 3. The Subject-Matter of Clergy Conferences

From the descriptive definition given above in Article 1, the material object of the clergy conferences centers in matters of moral theology and liturgy. Other exercises may be added by the ordinary if he judges them suitable for the promotion of knowledge and piety among the clergy.[17] Canon 131, § 1, seems to divide the subject-matter of the conferences into the necessary or obligatory and the voluntary or optional. The necessary or obligatory subject-matter calls for discussions on matters of moral theology and liturgy; the voluntary or optional subject-matter looks to discussions as determined by the ordinary.

The provision concerning the material object of the conferences is a codification of the legislation enacted by the synod of Benevento in the year 1693.[18] This synod of Benevento was the

[17] Can. 131, § 1.

[18] "Mandat Sancta Synodus ut in qualibet Provinciae civitate et foranea Vicaria semel in hebdomada sacrorum Rituum et conscientiae casuum congregatio iuxta methodum ab eadem approbatam et in Appendice apponendam, habeatur."—*Mansi,* XXIII, 458.

first to make express mention of discussions concerning liturgical cases or problems. The very same enactment was adopted by the Council of Rome held in the year 1725.[19] The Code of Canon Law now designates matters of moral theology and liturgy as the necessary or obligatory material object of clergy conferences in its universal legislation.

Canon 131, § 1, prescribes that the meetings be occupied with discussions "*de re morali et liturgica.*" Does this phrase refer to systematic treatments of the subjects in question? The entire history of the institute points to the fact that the conferences were very practical in nature and dealt with the solution of problems and cases. Likewise the words of canon 131, § 2, and of canon 591 do not point to such a scientific study. Canon 131, § 2, states that, if it be difficult to hold the meetings, then the solutions of cases should be prepared in writing according to norms established by the ordinary. Canon 591 demands that in the monthly conferences of religious a moral and a liturgical case shall be solved and, at the discretion of the superior, a sermon delivered on dogmatic and kindred subjects. The terms used in the canons, though generic in relation to the subjects themselves, suggest practical treatments on matters of moral theology and liturgy which lend themselves more readily to discussion, likewise, the very concept of a conference implies a discussion.[20]

It seems that with reference to the obligatory subject-matter of the conferences, there is now adopted an order of precedence which changes the order of the subjects mentioned in the synod of Benevento and in the Council of Rome (1725).[21] Canon 131, § 1, lists moral theology and liturgy as the necessary subject-matter of clergy conferences. Moral theology is that subsidiary branch of theology which treats of human acts in their supernatural relationship to the praise and possession of God, who exists as the Creator and as the Author of revelation.[22]

[19] Cf. *supra*, p. 29.

[20] Galasso, *De Cleri Collationibus*, p. 98.

[21] Cf. *supra*, p. 39, note 18.

[22] Busquet et Garcia-Bayon, *Thesaurus Confessarii* (10. ed., Matriti, 1940), p. 7; Genicot-Salsmans, *Institutiones Theologiae Moralis*, (11. ed.,

Thus any discussion, treatment, etc., which considers human acts in their theological-moral aspects finds relevance under the phrase "*de re morali.*" Liturgy may be defined as the science or study which treats of the public worship canonized by the Church.[23] Thus any exercise or discussion which deals with the sacred acts of worship, the rubrics, and the method of the administration of the sacraments faills within the scope of the phrase "*de re liturgica.*"

The necessary material object of the conferences is very extensive in itself and affords subject-matter in such a rich variety that all repetitiousness can readily be avoided. Usually, at least in the archdioceses and dioceses of the United States, the subject-matter of the conferences is determined by the chancery officials at the advice of the ordinary. Systematic arrangement of the material is preferable, but is not made necessary by the law itself. In fact, because of some particular problem in the diocese, a repeated discussion of the same material from various aspects may prove more desirable and profitable. The flexibility of the law in regard to clergy conferences should not be overlooked especially in respect to the subject-matter of the meetings.[24]

Would the provisions of the law on clergy conferences be fulfilled if the conferences were to deal only with dogmatic and liturgical problems? In such a case the law would seem to be only partially carried out, unless the dogmatic truth were also considered under the aspect of moral theology. This could readily be accomplished for the purpose of evoking the desired discussion of the matter. Besides, although the present writer has found no author or commentator who suggests that the sacred canons be considered in the solution of problems and cases, it seems almost impossible to give a complete solution without reference to Canon Law. For instance, practical discussions on the sacraments and clerical obligations, etc., certainly

---

Bruxellis, 1927), I, 7; Noldin-Schmitt, *Summa Theologiae Moralis,* (26. ed., 3 vols., Oeniponte: F. Rauch, 1940), I., n. 1.

23 Augustine [Bachofen], *Liturgical Law* (St. Louis: B. Herder. 1931), p. 1; P. Greco, *Compendio di Sacra Liturgia* (Lecco, 1922), p. 7.

24 Galasso, *De Cleri Collationibus,* pp. 97-100.

would not be profitable without a proper reference to the pertinent canons.

The forty-fifth decree of the XLI archdiocesan Synod of Milan, which was held in the year 1931, does not seem to be in accord with the provision of the law relative to the necessary subject-matter of the meetings. This decree lists the possible subjects of the conferences to be moral theology, exegetics, church history or liturgy. According to this list, liturgy is designated only as optional subject-matter, which appears to be contrary to the provision of canon 131, § 1.[25]

Besides the obligatory or necessary material object of the conferences, the law permits and suggests pertinent subjects which the ordinary judges opportune for advancing the learning and piety of the clergy.[26] The freedom of action afforded the bishop in the choice of these subjects is very extensive, so as to suggest and allow provision for particular needs and problems in the diocese. The law does not prescribe or determine any necessary or obligatory subject-matter for these exercises, nor does it hint at practical discussions, although these may be preferable. Many diocesan statutes carry specifications of the voluntary or optional matters to be discussed. For instance, the president of the conference may be obliged to present a summary of the recent acts and decrees of the Holy See.[27]

The optional or voluntary subject-matter of the conferences may consist of topics drawn from dogmatic, ascetical, mystical and pastoral theology, from Sacred Scripture, apologetics, church history, sacred eloquence, spiritual exercises, etc. Readings and considerations on the sacred canons are indeed most appropriate. However, as has been said above, the treatment of the necessary subject-matter already includes reference to the sacred canons.

[25] "In eam formam a S. Carolo praestitutam sex saltem quotannis Cleri congregationes tum in Civitate, tum in unoquoque Vicariatu Foraneo habeantur de re morali, exegetica, historia ecclesiastica, vel liturgica."—*Synodus Dioecesana Mediolanensis XLI*, (Mediolani, 1932), decr. 45.

[26] Can. 131, § 1.

[27] ". . . At these conferences he (the dean) shall give a summary of recent acts and decrees of the Holy See."—*Eighth Synod of Dubuque*, 1947, Statute no. 12; likewise, Statute no. 57, *Third Synod of Nashville*, 1947.

Theoretical treatises on the various subjects of theology contribute rather to the promotion of knowledge than to the spirituality of the clergy.

Many dioceses prescribe that a sermon be delivered by a designated priest or that a day of recollection accompany the conference.[28] Other prescriptions, designed to nourish the spiritual life of the participants of the conferences, include visits to the Most Blessed Sacrament. Benediction of the Most Blessed Sacrament, examination of conscience, recitation of the Rosary and other prayers in honor of the Blessed Virgin Mary, celebration of a High Mass for the souls of the faithful departed or for the deceased members of the clergy, etc.[29]

The III Plenary Council of Baltimore (1884) designated a case of conscience as the necessary or obligatory subject-matter of the meetings. It likewise provided for papers on Sacred Scripture, dogmatic theology, canon law, and liturgy.[30] The Code of Canon Law, on the other hand, prescribes specifically discussions only on moral theology and liturgy, permitting the ordinary to freely choose other pertinent subjects.[31] The provision of the Council is more comprehensive in scope when it demands the solution of a case of conscience and the treatment of other questions from various branches of theology. It seems justifiable to state that the provisions of Council are opposed to the Code of Canon Law and therefore must yield to the present universal law.[32] The Code of Canon Law seems to call for more than the solution of a case of conscience when it points to

[28] Galasso, *De Cleri Collationibus*, pp. 106-108.

[29] Galasso, *De Cleri Collationibus*, p. 108; also the *Statutes of the Archdiocese of Dubuque* as enacted in the Eighth Synod, held in 1947.

[30] "Casus conscientiae solutio ab omnibus qui coetui adesse debent, scriptis exaretur. . . . Aliis autem quaestionibus de Sacra Scriptura, Theologia Dogmatica, Jure Canonico, et Sacra Liturgia satisfiat ab iis quibus in antecedenti conventu praeses id curae demandaverit."—*Acta et Decreta*, no. 192.

[31] Can. 131, § 1.

[32] Can. 6, § 1; Barrett, *A Comparative Study of the Councils of Baltimore and the Code of Canon Law*, The Catholic University of America Canon Law Studies, n. 83 (Washington, D. C.: The Catholic University of America, 1932), p. 46.

the necessary subject-matter of the conferences as consisting of discussions "*de re morali et liturgica.*" Likewise, relative to the specified papers on questions of certain other subjects of theology, the III Plenary Council of Baltimore would at least partially circumscribe the area or extent of the bishop's choice. This seems clearly opposed to the liberty which the Code of Canon Law now grants in the words, "quibus addi possunt aliae exercitationes, quas Ordinarius opportunas iudicaverit ad scientiam et pietatem clericorum promovendam." [33]

In an Instruction (May 13, 1950, *De Scriptura Sacra recte docenda*), the Pontifical Biblical Commission suggested that an appropriate excerpt drawn from Holy Scripture be included in the discussions at all clergy conferences. This excerpt should be duly selected by the seminary Scripture professor.[34] This suggestion determines a phase of the optional subject-matter of the meetings, but is not opposed to the legislation of the Code of Canon Law. Besides, any diocesan measure designating the bishop's choice in regard to the optional matter of the discussions is warranted as long as it serves the promotion and the advancement of learning and piety among the clergy of the diocese.

[33] Can. 131, § 1; Barrett, *op. cit.*, p. 46.

[34] "Praeterea in collationibus seu conferentiis quae a clero saeculari quam regulari ad normam eiusdem Iuris canonici statis temporibus de re morali et liturgica habendae sunt, explicanda proponatur etiam—ut in quibusdam regionibus multa cum laude fit—pericopa aliqua biblica sive Veteris sive Novi Testamenti, quae a magistro rei biblicae Seminarii apte eligatur . . ." *AAS* XLII (1950), 568-578.

CHAPTER VI

THE ORGANIZATION OF CLERGY CONFERENCES

In the preceding chapter the nature, purpose and subject-matter of clergy conferences were dealt with. The present universal legislation in regard to the conferences affords only definite outlines and leaves much to particular rules and regulations. The specific determination of the place, the frequency and the procedure of the meetings rests, in great part at least, with the local ordinary. The local ordinary, therefore, is granted a great deal of freedom in adapting the conferences to the circumstances of his diocese.

Article 1. The Place of the Conferences

The Code of Canon Law designates explicitly the general territories wherein the conferences are to be convened.[1] It does not, however, mention the actual location of the meetings, for it simply states that the conferences are to be held in the episcopal city and in each rural deanery. This prescription was previously enacted by the I Provincial Council of Milan, which was held in the year 1565.[2]

Canon 131, § 1, divides the members of the secular clergy into two classes relative to the conferences. The clergy of the episcopal city convene within the city and the clergy of each deanery district gather somewhere in their local deanery. But the Code of Canon Law does not prohibit a priest who is stationed in the episcopal city from attending the meetings at another place, as long as he attends them within the boundaries of his proper diocese. Convenience would justify such attendance.

The law directly demands only that the conferences be convened in the episcopal city in each rural deanery. It is not

[1] Can. 131, § 1.

[2] Mansi, XXXIV, 42.

difficult to ascertain which city of the diocese is the episcopal one. The episcopal city is the city wherein the cathedral church is situated. Commonly this city is called the episcopal see.[3] The episcopal or diocesean see is erected by a special act reserved to the Holy See.[4] The episcopal city holds precedence over all the other cities of the diocese by reason of the location of the cathedral church, which is called the mother church of all the other churches in the diocese.

The episcopal city is the city wherein the local ordinary has his residence because of the location of the cathedral church. The term *Ordinarius* is to be considered not only in accordance with the norm of canon 329, § 1, but also according to canon 198, § 1. Canon 329, § 1, delineates, a local ordinary as a successor of the Apostles who has jurisdiction over a particular territory assigned to him by the Roman Pontiff, Canon 338, § 1, states that the ordinary must reside within the boundaries of his diocese. Accordingly, the term episcopal city must be understood as the place where the local ordinary resides by reason of the location of the cathedral church, whether he actually possess the episcopal character or not. The term *Ordinarius* of canon 198, § 1, includes abbots and prelates nullius, apostolic administrators, vicars and prefects apostolic, vicars general, or also those who supply for them and succeed them in office.

In regard to the vicar general, the law indicates that he cannot conduct conferences independently of the local bishop. The vicar general is obliged to notify the bishop of measures which have been or are to be taken as safeguards for the discipline of the clergy.[5] It cannot be denied that the universal law demanding the convocation of clergy conferences refers specifically to the discipline of the clergy. As a necessary consequence, the vicar general must consult the local bishop relative to any arrangements he might wish to make concerning the meetings commonly known as clergy conferences.

Vicars and prefects apostolic govern their mission territories with many rights and obligations of a ordinary of a diocese

3 Galasso, *De Cleri Collationibus*, p. 116.

4 Canons 215-217.

5 Can. 369, § 1.

with full canonical status. However, since mission territories do not enjoy the full canonical status of a diocese, there is no strict law demanding the holding of clergy conferences.[6]

The principal reason for the convening of the conferences in the episcopal city is the fact that the clergy there generally, as Ojetti stated excel in number and in status (in view of the important offices entrusted to them).[7] In fact, the number of the clergy in the episcopal city usually is greater than the number in any individual rural deanery, e.g., the seminary may be situated in the episcopal city. Besides, in consequence of the larger number of the priests in a restricted area and in view of the fact that some of them have received specialized training for the offices they hold, the meetings can be more readily convened and perhaps with greater success.

Furthermore, the conferences are to be held in each rural deanery of the diocese. According to the norm of canon 217, § 1, the term deanery signifies a part of district of the diocese as the result of a convenient division. Each deanery consists of a number of parishes in a given district, which in size may vary from diocese to diocese. The number of priests likewise varies from deanery to deanery. If it be impossible or inadvisable to divide the diocese into deaneries, the ordinary must consult the Holy See and abide by its decision.[8] This division of the diocese into deaneries is especially appropriate for the convoking of the conferences, since it allows the priests to attend near their parishes. Without this convenient division into deaneries, some priests might be obliged to travel a great distance or to be absent from their posts for an undesirable length of time.

A rural dean (*vicarius foraneus*) is placed over each deanery, and has special rights and corresponding duties.[9] The rural

[6] Can. 303.

[7] *Commentarium in Codicem Iuris Canonici* (4 vols., Romae: Apud Aedes Universitatis Gregorianae, 1927-1931), III, 101 (hereafter cited as *Commentarium*).

[8] " Si haec distributio ratione circumstantiarum, videatur impossibilis aut inopportuna, Episcopus consulat Sanctam Sedem, nisi ab eadem iam fuerit provisum."—Can. 217, § 2.

[9] Canons 445-450.

dean is obliged to summon the members of the clergy in his district to the conferences on the days designated by the local ordinary.[10] The Code of Canon Law does not prohibit as arrangement whereby the meetings are held in the various parishes of the deanery by turns. Accordingly the conferences can be convened in a place outside the parish of the dean. In fact, circumstances may warrant another location, e.g., greater facilities for accommodating the participants. It may of course become advisable to summon the priests to the residence of the dean, especially if it is situated in the center of the district.

In a survey of diocesan synods in Europe, Father Galasso found that two systems are followed in regard to the place of the conferences.[11] The first system determines a definite location for the meetings through diocesan legislation. The second system suggests that the conferences be held in the various parishes of the deanery in turn. In France, both systems are used. In Italy, the conferences are usually held in the various parishes of the deanery by turns. In the United States, it seems safe to state, the conferences are generally convened in the city or the parish where the dean resides.

There may obtain a third system, by which the meetings would be held in the various parishes of the deanery by turns, but for a definite duration of time, e.g., for two years in each parish successively. Besides, there is no provision of law, prohibiting a system whereby the meetings would at the same time be convened in two parishes of the deanery for the purpose of convenience, or because the large number of the participants, or because of the extensive size of the deanery. This possibility seems justified from canon 448, § 1, which states that the dean is to preside over the conferences held in his district.

It would seem contrary to the mind of the legislator if the members of two or more deaneries would convene in the same place for the conferences. The law requires that the meetings be held in each of the rural deaneries.[12] If local circumstances should warrant the gathering of priests from two or more dean-

[10] Can. 448, § 1.

[11] *De Cleri Collationibus*, pp. 118-120.

[12] Canon 131, § 1.

eries for the conferences, perhaps the most satisfactory solution would be the realignment of the districts into larger deaneries. The law does not prohibit a rearrangement of the deaneries whenever that seems advisable for good rasons.

In regard to clergy conferences, the episcopal city as the place for the holding of the meetings may include the suburban areas, although strictly taken the episcopal city is not a deanery. It is equivalently so considered, however, in accord with the division of the diocese prescribed in canon 217. The priests stationed in the episcopal city convene in a parish or place appointed as the location of the meetings, just as the priests in the deaneries convene in their appointed place.

The Code of Canon Law does not designate the actual place of the conferences; it simply states that the meetings are to be held in the episcopal city and in each rural deanery.[13] Therefore, the local ordinary determines, either himself or through his delegate, the actual meeting place of the conferences. The bishop can designate the specific location of the meetings by means of diocesan statute, or even a legitimately entrenched custom could point out the place of the meetings.

Article 2. The Time and Frequency of the Conferences

Section A. The Time of the Conferences

The Code of Canon Law again only affords a general and rather indefinite designation concerning the time when or the days on which the clergy conferences should be held. The law here permits the local ordinary to adapt the universal law to the particular circumstances of his diocese. It also prescribes that the meetings for the secular clergy are to be convened in the episcopal city and in each rural deanery or the days designated by the local ordinary.[14] Thus the time or the actual days of the meetings are to be set by the local ordinary, or at least with his approval. It is true that the bishop is empowered to delegate someone to establish the dates of the conferences, e.g.,

[13] Can. 131, § 1.

[14] Can. 131, § 1: "*diebus ab Episcopo designatis*"; and can. 448, § 1: "*diebus arbitrio Ordinarii loci praestituendis.*"

the rural dean, some representative, or even the entire group of the participants, as would be the case if the days of the meetings were selected by a common agreement of the participants. It appears from the very words of the canon, however, that a designation by the priests should always have the approval of the ordinary.[15] It must be remembered that the prior right to determine the dates of the meetings rests with the ordinary, and not with the rural dean. It is the duty of the rural dean to convoke the conferences on the days appointed by the ordinary.

Various councils and synods held in Europe have set the dates and even the exact hours of the meetings.[16] The Plenary Council of Calabria, which was held in the year 1934, enacted that the dates of the conferences should be set by the prefect or moderator of the conferences.[17]

At first sight it could seem that this enactment is expressly opposed to the general law of the Code, which requires the designation of the days for the meetings by the ordinary. But in the episcopal city the prefect or the moderator of the conferences is the ordinary himself. In the rural districts or deaneries, the deans can be designated by the ordinary to choose the days of the conferences, as long as the ordinary approves of the dates set by his delegates. It may here be noted that an enactment which grants the prefect or the moderator of the conferences the right to choose the dates may cause difficulties. For instance, could a bishop in his own person, contrary to the statute or enactment of such a council, designate the dates of the meetings once for all? It seems that he could do so, inasmuch as the law grants him this faculty expressly.[18]

The decrees of a provincial council, as well as of a plenary council, are only the common enactments of a number of bishops. It is true that these decrees require inspection and recognition from the Holy See, but only as a condition for their legitimate promulgation. This recognition gives them no further positive

15 Can. 131, § 1; can. 448, § 1.

16 Galasso, *De Cleri Collationibus*, pp. 133-135.

17 *Ibid.*, p. 134.

18 Canons 131, § 1 and 448, § 1.

authority from the Holy See.[19] It can be objected that the enactments and decrees of a provincial or plenary council, once they are promulgated, bind in the entire territory of the province or the country. The individual ordinaries can dispense from these laws only in particular instances and with a just cause.[20] Measures enacted by a council cannot derogate from the law of the Code. If they do, they are not valid enactments. Since canon 131, § 1, and canon 448, § 1, grant the ordinary express power to choose the dates of the conferences, no particular law can deprive him of the power which the universal law grants him. Canon 448, § 1, appoints the rural dean as the prefect or the moderator of the meetings in his district or deanery, but it likewise states expressly that he is to convene the gatherings not on his own authority but on the days designated by the local ordinary.

SECTION B. THE FREQUENCY OF THE CONFERENCES

The requirement concerning the frequency of the clergy conferences is simply stated in the Code of Canon Law by means of the phrase, "*saepius in anno*".[21]. There is much discussion among the authors and commentators about the required frequency of the meetings. There is also much discrepancy concerning the precise meaning of *saepius in anno*. In attempting to determine an exact numerical figure to fulfill the law, the authors and commentators prefer to suggest that the conferences be held from at least two to twelve times a year.[22]

19 Can. 291, § 1; Cf. *AAS,* XIII (1921), 228.

20 Can. 291, § 2.

21 Can. 131, § 1.

22 "About two or three times a year"—Charles Augustine, *A Commentary on the New Code of Canon Law* (8 vols., Vol. I, 3. ed., 1920; Vol. II, 3. ed., 1919; Vol. III, 2. ed., 1919, St. Louis: B. Herder Book Co.), II, 76; "quater saltem"—Blat, *Commentarium,* II, *De Personis,* Pars I, n. 68; "saltem quater vel quinquies, melius si frequentius"—Cappello, *Summa Iuris Canonici* (3 vols., Vol. I, 4. ed., Romae: Apud Aedes Universitatis Gregorianae, 1945), I, n. 233; "saltem sexies in anno"—Matthaeus Conte a Coronata, *Institutiones Iuris Canonici* (5 vols., Vol. I, 4. ed., 1950; Vol. II, 3. ed., 1947, Romae: Marietti), I, n. 190; "fere quolibet mense"—Guidus Cocchi, *Commentarium in Codicem Iuris Canonici* (8 vols., Vol. I, 6. ed.,

Zaplotnik points out that five or six times a year can definitely be considered as *saepius*, but he likewise comes to the conclusion that twice a year can be sufficient if local and particular circumstances are taken into account.[23] Other authors and commentators refrain from stating the definite number of the conferences that would satisfy the meaning of "saepius in anno."[24]

Father Galasso in his treatise on clergy conferences reaches the conclusion that the conferences must be held at least twelve times a year.[25] He places considerable emphasis on stating canon 591 as parallel to canon 131. Canon 591 prescribes and delineates conferences for religious in their own houses at least once a month.[26]

1947; Vol. II, 4. ed., 1937; Vol. IV, 4. ed., 1946; Vol. VIII, 4. ed., 1938, Taurinorum Augustae: Marietti), II, 111; Goyeneche, *Iuris Canonici Summa Principia* (Romae, 1935), p. 165; "fere semel in mense"—P. Maroto, *Institutiones Iuris Canonici* (2 vols., Vol. I, 3. ed., Romae: Apud Commentarium pro Religiosis, 1921), I, 562; "regulariter eam vocem accipiendam quatenus tres saltem requirat coetus cogendos"—Ojetti, Commentarium, III, 101; "videtur sufficere si Ordinarius praescribat huiusmodi conferentias quolibet mense"—D. Pruemmer, *Manuale Theologiae Moralis* (3 vols., 8. ed., Friburgi Brisgoviae: Herder & Co., 1935-1936), II, p. 89, nota 7; "videtur fieri satis, si semel in mense aut duodecim conferentiae singulis annis"—*Wernz-Vidal,* II, n. 137.

23 "Quinquies vel sexies in anno certe saepius est. Si ipsum verbum "saepe" vel "saepius" solum excogitetur, ter vel quater videtur esse minimum ut lege satisfiat; si vero difficultates aliquorum locorum et temporum ponderentur, tum "saepe" bis exaequare potest."—*De Vicariis Foraneis* (Catholica Universitas Americae, Washingtonii, 1927), p. 114.

24 Cesar Badii, *Institutiones Iuris Canonici* (3. ed., 2 vols., Florentiae: Libreria Editrice Florentina, 1921-1922), II, n. 193; Alphonsus De Meester, *Iuris Canonici et Iuris Canonico-Civilis Compendium* (4 vols., Vol. I, nova ed., Brugis: Sumptibus et Typis Societatis Sancti Augustini, 1921), I, n. 362; E. Eichmann—K. Moersdorf, *Lehrbuch des Kirchenrechts auf Grund des Codex Iuris Canonici* (6. ed., 3 vols., Paderborn: Schoeningh, 1949-1950), I, n. 44; Gerardus Oesterle, *Praelectiones Iuris Canonici* (Vol. I, Romae, 1931), I, 75; Vermeersch-Creusen, *Epitome Iuris Canonici* (3 vols., Vol. I, 7. ed., 1949; Vol. III, 6. ed., 1946, Mechlinae-Romae: H. Dessain), I, n. 250.

25 Haec nostra est in re sententia, nempe legi collationum non satisfieri nisi collationes habeantur in anno saltem duodecim" *De Cleri Collationibus,* p. 141.

26 . . . "minimum semel in mense."

This parallelism is hardly sustainable. First of all, the words employed in the two canons are not the same. The phrase "*minimum semel in mense*" of canon 591 is, furthermore, certainly definite, whereas the "*saepius in anno*" of canon 131 is indefinite. Accordingly no parallelism can be claimed. Moreover, the legislation of canon 131 extends not only to all secular priests but also to many religious. Canon 591 refers to fully integrated houses of religious (domus formatae) only, and the very circumstances of the two laws are greatly different.[27] It is definitely more difficult for the members of the secular clergy and for the religious who are bound to attend the conferences prescribed in canon 131 than it is for the religious in fully integrated houses to gather for the meetings described in canon 591. Father Galasso states it as his opinion that the legislator had the same intention in formulating the two laws in regard to the number of the conferences.[28]

This doctrine of Father Galasso hardly seems tenable. The legislator could easily have used the same terms. Furthermore, the second paragraph of canon 131 gives an alternative if it is difficult to hold the conferences for seculars, whereas canon 591 insists that the conferences in religious houses be convened at least once each month, and allows no alternative for fewer meetings. It is manifest that the difficulties involved in convening the secular clergy for the meetings are far greater than those involved in gathering the religious of a particular house, since all reside there in common.

Father Galasso goes on to make reference to previous legislation in regard to the frequency of the conferences. He argues that in virtue of canon 6, n. 4, one must consider the previous law when the present law remains obscure. Since the previous legislation prescribed the conferences as often as 48 times a year, and since the present law simply states "*saepius in anno*" in regard to the frequency of the conferences, certainly one cannot

[27] Canons 131 and 591.

[28] "Novimus pro Religiosis praescribi collationes 'minimum semel in mense'; quibus ex verbis apparet, seu melius deduci potest quod si Legislator vult ut apud Religiosos collationes saltem duodecies in anno fiant, non aliam esse intentionem eius putandum est quoad numerum collationum cleri saecularis . . ."—*op. cit.*, p. 141.

reduce the number to six, five, four, three or even two a year.[29]

It seems that Father Galasso places too much stress upon the fact that the previous legislation designated the exact number of the conferences within a particular period of time. e.g., the Council of Rome which was held in 1725 required weekly meetings.[30] The present universal law seems to legislate something quite different from the earlier particular enactments. Instead of requiring a set number of the conferences in a short period of time, e.g., once a month or once a week, the Code of Canon Law simply points to "*saepius in anno*" as the norm for the frequency of the meetings.[31] The law now contains an indefinite measure in regard to the number of the conferences, and the temporal designation is a year. Thus the length of time is sufficiently long to allow for local conditions and circumstances in satisfying the prescription of the law regarding the frequency of convening the clergy conferences. In other words, the present universal law ordains only an indefinite norm, quite distinct from the former precise particular enactments concerning the frequency of clergy conferences.

The repeated petitions wherein the French and German bishops requested the Holy See in the nineteenth century for a universal law on conferences for the clergy, both groups sug-

29 "Si praeterea canones qui ex parte tantum cum veteri jure congruunt, qua congruunt, ex jure antiquo aestimandi sunt; qua discrepant, sunt ex sua ipsorum sententia dijudicandi; et in dubio num aliquod canonum praescriptum cum veteri jure discrepet, a veteri jure non est recedendum; omne dubium quoad interpretationem expressionis 'saepius in anno' effugabitur, si ad jus vetus attendamus. Jamvero in veteri jure, sicut in plurimis Conciliis et Synodis statutum fuisse vidimus, collationes generatim pluries in mense haberi praescriptum erat; quod si tamen Codex noluit numerum conferentiarum determinare, et tantum dixit 'saepius in anno' habendas esse, non potest certo ita a veteri jure recedi ut dum antea habebantur ex. gr. per 48 vices in anno, nuc [sic] vero ad sex, quinque, quatuor, tres, vel etiam duas, collationes reducantur."—*De Cleri Collationibus*, p. 141.

30 "Congregationes tum in Civitatibus, tum in Dioecesibus . . . semel in unaquaque hebdomada, certoque designando die . . ."—*Coll. Lacensis*, I, col. 371. Likewise the Provincial Synod of Benevento, held in the year 1693, and the Provincial Synod of Naples, held in the year 1699, both required weekly conferences.

31 Can. 131, § 1.

gested a precise and definite number.[32] In their requests, the French bishops designated that the meetings be called at least six or seven times a year. The bishops of Germany felt that the conferences should be convened even more frequently—once every two weeks, or at least once a month. The present universal law did make the meetings obligatory, but manifestly did not want to set any precise number for the conferences when it employed the indefinite expression "*saepius in anno.*"

The phrase "*saepius in anno*" of canon 131, § 1, is sometimes translated in English as several times a year.[33] Woywod prefers to translate it as repeatedly,[34] and Ramstein stated that the conferences would be held frequently (*saepius*) every year.[35] Augustine admitted that the phrase "*saepius in anno*" indicated the number of the meetings only approximately, but added that this expression is to be interpreted as calling for about two or three meetings a year.[36] He referred to one of the sayings (*Dictio*) of Barbosa, namely that "*saepius*" regularly means three times, but sometimes can mean twice.[37] This interpretation of the word "*saepius*" could prove acceptable in itself, but since canon 131, § 1, it is to be considered in relation to a temporal terminus as set in the modifying phrases "*in anno*", the present law is indeterminate enough in itself to allow for consideration of local conditions and circumstances.

Thus the study of the authors and commentators in regard to the frequency of the conferences leaves much to be desired. The phrase "*saepius in anno*" is in itself indefinite, so that it

32 *Coll. Lac.*, VII, col. 834; cf. also col. 873.

33 John A. Abbo–Jerome D. Hannon, *The Sacred Canons* (2 vols., St. Louis: B. Herder Book Co., 1952), I, 85; T. L. Bouscaren–A. C. Ellis, *A Text and Commentary* (2. printing, Milwaukee, Wis.: The Bruce Publishing Co., 1948), p. 110.

34 A Practical Commentary on the Code of Canon Law (10. printing, 2 vols., revised by Callistus Smith, New York: Joseph F. Wagner, Inc., 1946), I, n. 100.

35 *A Manual of Canon Law* (Hoboken, N. J.: Terminal Printing and Publishing Co., 1947), p. 176.

36 *A Commentary on the New Code of Canon Law,* II, 76.

37 "Saepius, quandoque duabus vicibus contentatur, regulariter tamen tres requirit actus."—*Tractatus Varii,* Dictio 362, p. 786, as cited by Augustine.

permits particular legislation to adapt the general law to territorial circumstances.[38] This seems to be the very intention of the law itself. It also seems necessary to consider the phrase "*saepius in anno*" in relation to the second paragraph of canon 131, which substitutes written solutions in place of the meetings if it is difficult to hold the conferences. This substitution for the actual conferences definitely seems invoked as a last resort.

It is true that if the conferences cannot be held "*saepius in anno*" as demanded by the first paragraph of canon 131, then the means prescribed in the second paragraph, namely written solutions, is to be resorted to. But since "*saepius in anno*" is a relative term, what may be "*saepius in anno*" in one diocese, e.g., four times a year, may be an impossible regulation in another diocese because of local conditions and circumstances. The question may be asked: If the conferences are convened actually only once a year with good reason, should the ordinary also demand written solutions of the priests at another time during the year in order to comply with the law of "*saepius in anno*"? It seems that he should prescribe written solutions once during the year in addition to the convocation of the meetings once a year. The law seems to prefer actual meetings to written solutions; the latter it proposes only as a final resort.[39] Thus also, if because of the circumstances in a particular diocese the conferences are convened twice a year, it seems safe to conclude that the law concerning the frequency of the meetings would be fulfilled, so that no additional written solutions would need to be prescribed.

In the United States, the decrees of the III Plenary Council of Baltimore (1884) must be taken into consideration, since this Council legislated about the frequency of the conferences. The Council prescribed at least four meetings in the course of the year in the cities, and two meetings each year in the rural districts.[40] Can the decrees of the III Plenary Council of Balti-

[38] Ryan, *Principles of Episcopal Jurisdiction*, pp. 117–139.

[39] Can. 131, § 1 and § 2.

[40] "Pro civitatibus ad quas facilis patet aditus, quater saltem in anno, in districtibus vero ruralibus, ubi in unum locum venire difficilius esset, bis in anno, huiusmodi collationes ecclesiasticae habeantur."—*Acta et Decreta*, no. 192.

more concerning the number of the conferences still stand as an appropriate interpretation of the present law of canon 131? Barrett maintains that, "our more definite local statute requiring at least each year four in cities gives a satisfactory interpretation and determination to the common law and continues to be our rule." [41] It certainly seems safe to conclude that this enactment still binds in our country as a proper determination of the "*saepius in anno*" of canon 131.

Relative to the Council's prescription of two conferences per year, Barrett states:

> "As for the two a year allowed by the Council for rural districts the same can hardly be said. The Code makes no distinction between the city and the country and so the word *saepius* applies to both. Twice a year can hardly be considered often and so it would seem that this indulgence on the part of the Council is opposed to the Code and can no longer be availed of without the permission of the Holy See or the use of *epikeia*." [42]

It is true that the present Code of Canon Law does not distinguish between the cities and the rural districts in regard to the frequency of the conferences in its use of the phrase "*saepius in anno*," but it also seems true that such a distinction is not altogether precluded.[43] If the canon stated that the conferences must be held a definite number of times in the episcopal city and in each rural district of deanery, then the use of a distinction in one and the same territory would now be *contra ius*. But since the phrase "*saepius in anno*" is a relative one, and since there are always greater attendant difficulties in gathering together the priests of a rural district than in convening the priests in cities, the invoking of a distinction does not seem contrary to the present general law.

Thus it seems reasonable to maintain that the prescription of the III Council of Baltimore [44] designating the conferences four times a year in the cities and twice a year in the rural districts complies with the present Code law. Bouscaren and Ellis seem

[41] *A Comparative Study of the Councils of Baltimore and the Code of Canon Law*, p. 46.

[42] *Loc. cit.*

[43] Can. 131, § 1.

[44] *Acta et Decreta*, no. 192.

to adhere to this designation concerning the law of Baltimore although they do not state it explicitly.[45] The special difficulties of convocation in the rural districts are occasioned by the distance to be traveled, by the necessity of absenting oneself from the parish for a longer period of time, and by other similar weighty considerations. It would likewise hardly be justifiable to substitute written solutions if the meetings can be convened at least twice a year. Consultation and approval of the Holy See does not appear necessary if the rule of the III Plenary Council of Baltimore is followed in our country, nor is the employment of the principle of *epikeia* a necessary resort for remaining within the framework of the Code's law.

Article 3. The Procedure in Clergy Conferences

Another circumstance to be considered is the procedure in or organization of the conferences. The present universal legislation allows the local ordinary to determine the formalities and the procedure in the meetings. The Code of Canon Law indicates that the Ordinary is to preside at the conferences in the episcopal city and that the rural dean (vicar forane) is to be the moderator or the prefect at the meetings held in his district or deanery on the days appointed by the ordinary.[46]

The law indirectly requires that definite rules of procedure be set up in each diocese regarding the conferences. This seems clearly to be implied in the words of the second paragraph of canon 448, wherein it is stated that, if the meetings are held in more than one place in the deanery, the moderator or the prefect has the duty to see to it that the conferences are properly held.[47]

In the absence of a definite schedule of dates for the meetings, the rural dean can draw up such a schedule only with consent of the ordinary. Without the consent, or at least the approval, of the ordinary, such meetings when convoked by the dean cannot be called clergy conferences in the strict sense of the word, for canon 448, § 1, clearly conditions the exercise of

[45] *Commentary*, p. 111.

[46] Canons 131 and 448.

[47] ". . . ubi vero plures habeantur huiusmodi coetus in variis districtus locis, invigilare [vicarius foraneus debet] ut rite celebrentur."—Can. 448, § 1.

the rural dean's authority in this regard upon the designation of the dates of the actual meetings by the local ordinary.[48] Thus a priest would not be bound to attend such gatherings when called by the rural dean without the authorization of the ordinary, since his obligation attaches only to clergy conferences in the strict sense of the term.[49] Likewise, the penalties stated and implied in canon 2377 could not be imposed upon such a priest for non-attendance. All penalties must be interpreted strictly,[50] and thus the penalties delineated in canon 2377 refer only to a refusal to attend the clergy conferences as outlined in the Code of Canon Law.[51]

The second paragraph of canon 131 requires the submitting of the written solutions to questions according to the norms established by the local ordinary only if it is difficult to convene actual meetings. It seems warranted to assume that the necessary and obligatory subject-matter to be demanded in these written solutions is the same as that of the actual conferences, namely, matter relating to moral theology and liturgy.[52] Likewise, the optional or voluntary matter of the written solutions is to deal with other subjects which the ordinary deems conducive to the learning and piety of the clergy.[53]

Written solutions of announced questions are required only when the prescribed conferences cannot be convened because of extant difficulties.[54] The law here demands more than ordinary difficulties. In fact, every law imposes at least some measure of inconvenience and its fulfillment is accompanied with ordinary difficulties. Sometimes the law itself establishes an alternative in the face of special difficulties which may arise. The law here considered is a case in point.[55]

[48] *The Jurist,* VII (1947), 88.

[49] *Loc. cit.*

[50] Can. 19.

[51] " Sacerdotes contra praescriptum can. 131, § 1, contumaces."

[52] Cf. can. 131, § 1.

[53] *Apollinaris,* XXIII (1950), 225.

[54] Can. 131, § 2.

[55] Can. 131, § 1 and § 2.

The second paragraph of canon 131 seems to relax the severity of the first paragraph by providing that, if it is difficult to hold these conferences, the solution of the cases shall be sent in according to the norms established by the local ordinary.[56] If the actual meetings can be convened only once a year, it seems necessary that the ordinary should at least at some other time during the year require written solutions in fulfillment of the law in regard to the holding of the conferences "*saepius in anno.*"

Special hardships which may militate against the actual convening of the meetings might include the required traveling of a great distance, the notable penury of the clergy, etc. The local ordinary is to judge whether the difficulties are such as to warrant an excuse from the convening of the actual meetings. Only when such difficulties exist should he employ the alternative given in the law to replace the actual convening of the conferences.[57] The rural dean could not dispense from the actual gatherings apart from at least a previous consultation with the ordinary, for the law requires that he convoke the meetings in his district or deanery on the days assigned by the local ordinary.[58] If the meetings cannot be convoked at any time during the year because of local difficulties and adverse circumstances, then written solutions are to be required at least twice each year in fulfillment of the law which demands that "*saepius in anno*" the conferences be held.[59]

The law envisages that ordinarily the conferences shall consist of essentially oral discussions on questions designated beforehand, as the very word conference implies. Nevertheless many plenary and provincial councils and diocesan synods propose that written solutions of cases and questions be furnished by some or all of the participants.[60] The III Plenary Council of Baltimore (1884) required written solutions, of a case of con-

[56] *The Jurist*, VII (1947), 88.

[57] Can. 131, § 2.

[58] Can. 448, § 1.

[59] Can. 131, § 1.

[60] Galasso, *De Cleri Collationibus*, p. 157.

science from all the participants who under obligation attended the conferences.[61]

This enactment seems to restrict the necessary or obligatory subject-matter of the conferences.[62] Yet, if one considers this measure in itself in the light of the present universal legislation, it would seem still to bind since a case of conscience certainly deals with a matter which is included in the phrase, "*de re morali et liturgica.*"[63] In treating of the laws of the Councils of Baltimore, legitimate custom must also be taken into account to ascertain whether the measures of this particular legislation retain their force. The present writer has failed to find more than three dioceses in this country which follow this dictate of the III Plenary Council of Baltimore. A great number of dioceses do not require any written solutions. A number of dioceses require the handing-in of written solutions but require more than the solution of the case of conscience. Thus it seems reasonable to conclude that the force of legitimate custom has obliterated the continued binding impetus of this enactment of the III Plenary Council of Baltimore or at least there is now a doubt that it still binds; therefore the measure appears to be devoid of force any longer.

The number of dioceses require the submission of written solutions by reason of diocesan statute since the promulgation of the Code of Canon Law. It cannot be concluded that these particular measures are contrary to the present universal law and therefore do not have any binding force. These enactments are rather to be considered as *praeter legem*—demanding more than the present law prescribes but not contrary or opposed to it.[64] Furthermore, also, a particular law containing exemptions for some of the participants would be valid and have full force of particular law, for example, the exemption for silver

[61] "Casus conscientiae solutio ab omnibus qui coetui adesse debent, scriptis exaretur."—*Acta et Decreta*, no. 192.

[62] Supra, pp. 43 ff.; Barrett, *A Comparative Study of the Councils of Baltimore and the Code of Canon Law*, p. 46.

[63] *The Jurist*, VII (1947), 89.

[64] Barrett, *op. cit.*, pp. 20-22.

jubilarians, etc.[65] If one of the priests who are obliged to attend the meetings is legitimately excused, written solutions can still be required of him by diocesan statute.[66] The Provincial Council of Portland (1932) prescribed that the rural dean collect the papers immediately after the close of the conference and relay them to the chancery office.[67] Many archdioceses and dioceses of Europe demand written answers and treatises from all the participants regardless of office or age.[68]

It is very desirable that each diocese have a suitable and convenient library with appropriate sources and reference books for the conferences. Without this convenience it will be quite difficult for the priests to properly prepare the material designated for the meetings. It is true, of course, that each priest should have a private library to care for his general needs, but often special references are necessary for the satisfactory preparation of a specific discussion.[69]

Once the meeting has been convened, several questions may be considered. First of all, what order of precedence is to be followed in the seating of the members of the conference? It seems that the order of precedence outlined in the law of the Code should be observed.[70] This order of precedence seems to be the more reasonable and consonant with the canonical precedence which is prescribed for public functions. It may be objected that the discussions in these meetings do not evince a public function wherein the clergy engages as a collegiate body. To this one may reply that, whether the function be public or private, the conference must be judged not from the place in

[65] *Synodus Dioecesana Eriensis Septima, 1947, Acta et Decreta,* no. 9; *First Synod of the Diocese of Scranton, 1949, Acta et Statuta,* no. 4: " Omnes qui decimum quintum annum sacerdotii non compleverunt Moderatori conferentiae, Adm. Rev. do Decano, scriptam casus conscientiae solutionem tradant, etiamsi legitime absentes fuerint."

[66] *First Synod of the Diocese of Scranton, 1949, Acta et Statuta, De Clericis,* no. 4.

[67] *Acta et Decreta,* n. 84.

[68] Galasso, *De Cleri Collationibus,* p. 158 and p. 159.

[69] Galasso, *De Cleri Collationibus,* p. 160.

[70] Can. 106.

which it is held but from the nature of the act itself. Since the meeting is concerned not only with matters relative to the direction of souls and other moral issues, but also with the fulfillment of an obligation prescriped by law for all clerics, it cannot be denied that the conference is public and must be considered as such. It must be admitted that a reasonable cause would exempt the members from following the order of precedence. In the United States, unfortunately, the order of precedence is generally overlooked.

The second question refers to the moderator of the president of the meetings. The Code of Canon Law does not state expressly that the ordinary is the president of the conferences held in the episcopal city, but it cannot be denied that he is. The ordinary can delegate someone else to preside, e.g., the vicar general or the pastor of the cathedral. He can designate him for each meeting, or assign him once for all. It would also be within the law to appoint several delegates who would preside at the meetings in turn.

The Code of Canon Law expressly states that the rural dean is to preside at the meetings in his district.[71] If, because of local circumstances, the conferences are held in several places of the same deanery, the dean can delegate another priest to take his place at the other meetings in the rôle of moderator. The dean's delegate is responsible to the dean and is to report to him regarding the fulfillment of the duties entrusted to him.

If the rural dean should accidentally be absent from the conferences, the order of precedence could reasonably indicate the temporary conductor or moderator of the meeting. This order of precedence would have to yield to any specific appointment made by the ordinary. The order of precedence would point to the senior pastor first according to dignity, then in ordination, and finally seniority by reason of age.[72]

The rights and duties of the rural dean in regard to the conferences as outlined in the Code of Canon Law obligate him:

1) to call the priests of his deanery or district to the conferences on the days set by the local ordinary;

[71] Can. 448, § 1.

[72] Can. 106, n. 3.

2) to preside at the meetings or, in the event that conferences are convened simultaneously in more than one place in his deanery, to see to it that the meetings are properly moderated;
3) to perform the special duties dictated by diocesan statute, e.g., to give a short summary of the recent acts and decrees of the Holy See regarding the clergy and laity.[73]

As moderator or president of the meetings, the rural dean or his substitute is obliged to:

1) open the meeting with a prayer or some prescribed spiritual exercise;
2) grant or deny permission to a participant to give his views in the discussions;
3) indicate when a question or case on the agenda of the meeting is sufficiently explored and discussed, and then point out at least in outline, the next prescribed question or problem for discussion.

Diocesan statutes may assign him further duties, such as the duty

1) to relay written solutions for the questions to the local ordinary as soon as possible;
2) to send in the names of the absent members to the ordinary with the reasons and excuses for their absence;
3) to give an account, at least annually, concerning the material in the ledger of the conferences by listing the place, date, hour and month of the meetings, by recounting which members were present, by indicating which members were absent along with the reasons for their absence, by noting which matters were discussed, etc.
4) to affix his signature to the acts drawn up by the secretary;
5) to appoint or to select a competent priest to supervise the actual discussions;
6) to notify the ordinary of the place, the day and the hour of the meeting several days in advance.[74]

[73] Cf. *Statutes of the Archdiocese of Dubuque, 1947,* no. 38; *Statutes of the Diocese of Nashville, 1947,* no. 57.

[74] Galasso, *De Cleri Collationibus,* pp. 163, 164.

Since the moderator or the president of the conferences cannot conveniently perform all the duties that call for performance, very many synods and diocesan statutes include among his functions the appointment of a secretary for the meetings.[75] The office of secretary relative to clergy conferences was already expressly mentioned in the Council of Rome (1725).[76] Nevertheless, to have someone serve specifically as the secretary is not strictly required by the Code of Canon Law. If a secretary is appointed, he is designated by the local ordinary for the meetings in the episcopal city and in each rural deanery. The local ordinary may permit the rural dean to appoint the secretary, or allow the selection to be made by the participants.[77] The duties of the secretary can be noted under the following two headings:

1) to record the minutes of the meetings along with the texts and summaries of the discussions, to record the names of the absent members and to note the causes or reasons of their absence, to record the names of the members chosen as leaders of the discussion on the assigned topics, and to note the decisions of the moderator;
2) to submit a written account of the above-mentioned agenda to the local ordinary at a designated time.[78]

In regard to the manner of selecting the members for conducting the discussions on the questions assigned, three different systems can be followed. The first designates the leaders by lot at the beginning of each year, so that they conduct the discussions in their turn. The second system suggests that the order of precedence be followed in the leading of the discussions. The third system suggests a more flexible order chosen by the moderator or the prefect.[79]

The III Plenary Council of Baltimore (1884) prescribed that two names be chosen by lot, and the members thus designated were to read their answers and to discuss the case of con-

[75] Galasso, *op. cit.*, p. 164.

[76] *Coll. Lac.*, I, col. 423.

[77] Galasso, *op. cit.*, p. 165.

[78] Galasso, *op. cit.*, p. 165.

[79] Galasso, *op. cit.*, p. 166.

science.[80] Regarding the other papers prescribed by the council, the moderator or the prefect could choose them at the previous meeting.[81]

Do these provisions of procedure at the conferences still bind for our country? As has been noted before, the subject-matter of the conferences has been changed by the present law.[82] On the other hand, as points of procedure these enactments could stand, but it seems safe to assert that custom has brought about a doubt of law in this regard, and therefore these prescriptions cease to bind.[83]

The order of business of a clergy conference might well include the following:

1) the opening prayer, spiritual exercise, etc., preferably invoking the Holy Spirit for His guidance;
2) the roll call and the reading of the minutes of the previous meeting by the moderator of the secretary;
3) the procedural program designated by the diocesan chancery, or by the moderator, usually outlined in Latin, with an appropriate discussion of the topics assigned;
4) the close of the discussion with summarized conclusions given by the moderator or the leader of the discussion;
5) the reading of the designated treatises which the local ordinary judges conducive to the learning and the piety of the clergy;
6) the miscellaneous business pertaining to the particular district or deanery;
7) the close of the meeting with prayer or some spiritual exercise, e.g., a visit in common to the Most Blessed Sacrament, etc.

80 "Duo, quorum nomina sortito exiverunt ex urna continente schedulas, in quibus omnes inscripti fuere, responsa sua legant et casum discutiant."—*Acta et Decreta,* no. 192.

81 "Aliis autem quaestionibus de Sacra Scriptura, Theologia Dogmatica, Iure Canonico, et Sacra Liturgia satisfiat ab iis quibus in antecedenti conventu praeses id curae demandaverit."—*Acta et Decreta,* no. 192.

82 Cf. *supra,* pp. 43 and 44.

83 Cf. can. 27 and also can. 15.

It is to be noted here that the mere reading of the papers assigned apart from all discussions on the practical level could hardly be called conferences in the strict sense of the term. The very word conference implies a meeting for formal consultation or discussion with an interchange of views. But a short paper read by the leader of the discussion, when he simply states the principles and the views relative to the topics concerned, may readily facilitate and provoke a profitable practical discussion. The reading of papers alone would amount equivalently to the presentation of so many lectures; it would lack the essential elements of the desired conference as contemplated in the law.

CHAPTER VII

THE OBLIGATION OF HOLDING AND ATTENDING CLERGY CONFERENCES

A study of the institute of clergy conferences and of the present legislation regarding them would not be complete without an exploration of the obligation that looks to the convening of these conferences and the consequent attendance thereat. Hence, in regard to diocesan clergy conferences, a triple aspect of the obligation can be considered; a) the obligation of convening the meetings, which binds the local ordinary and the rural dean; b) the obligation of presence and participation in the meetings and discussions, and c) the obligation on the part of the local ordinary and the rural dean to substitute written papers if the actual gatherings cannot be held because of adverse circumstances.

Article 1. The Obligation of Convening the Conferences

The very words of the law with reference to the convening of the conferences impose a true and proper obligation.[1] The law states that the meetings are to be held in the episcopal city and in each rural deanery.[2] Likewise, the substitution prescribed in case it is difficult to convene the conferences is also of an obligatory character and confirms the obligation for the convocation itself.[3]

The authors and commentators except Leitner are unanimous in stating that the obligation of holding the meetings is a real one.[4] Leitner admits that it is the heartfelt wish of the

[1] Can. 131, § 1.

[2] "In civitate episcopali et in singulis vicariatibus foraneis . . . conventus habeantur, quos collationes seu conferentiae vocant."—Can. 131, § 1.

[3] "Si conventus haberi difficile sit, resolutae quaestiones mittantur . . . ." Also, "Conventui interesse, aut, deficiente conventu, scriptam casuum solutionem mittere debent."—Can. 131, § 2 and § 3.

[4] "Wenn auch der Kodex keine eigentliche Pflicht aufstellt . . . ."—*Handbuch des katholischen Kirchenrechts* (5 Lieferungen in 2 Bände, Regensburg, 1918-1927), I, 227.

Church that the conference be convened, but at the same time denies that the present universal legislation imposes a true and real obligation concerning the holding of the meetings.[5] This opinion, as stated by Leitner, appears to have no foundation in law. The Code of Canon Law does not advise, but makes the conferences preceptive and obligatory. The subjunctive employed in canon 131 and 448 has the force of an imperative which fully denotes an obligation. The word " debet " in canon 448 unquestionably implies a true obligation.

An even more convincing argument for the presence of a strict obligation can be found in the penal canon which invokes a telling sanction for compliance with the obligation of individual attendance.[6] If the conferences were not obligatory in themselves, there could be no strict obligation of attendance, nor could there be any punishment for non-attendance. Moreover, *latae* or *ferendae sententiae* penalties are devised only for delinquents, namely for those who are violators of some law or precept. In the present case, the law for which canon 2377 invokes its sanction is expressly mentioned, i.e., canon 131, § 1.[7]

The authors and commentators simply state that the conferences are prescribed—meaning, of course, that the obligation of convening the meetings derives from the law itself. Some of them explicitly mention the obligation, while others only refer to it implicitly.[8] Father Galasso also makes a survey and lists various councils and synods which portray the real obligation for the convocation of the meetings.[9]

The nature of the obligation concerning the convening of the

[5] " . . . dass der Kirche die Abhaltung dieser Konferenz eine Herzensangelegenheit ist."—*Ibid.*, p. 228.

[6] Can. 2377.

[7] " Sacerdotes contra praescriptum can. 131, § 1 contumaces, Ordinarius pro suo prudenti arbitrio puniat . . . . "

[8] " Nunc primo lege generali faciendae praescribuntur."—Coronata, *Compendium Iuris Canonici*, I, n. 382; cf. also Galasso, *De Cleri Collationibus*, p. 175, note 1.

[9] *De Cleri Collationibus*, p. 175, note 2; also cf. *Quarta (et Quinta) Synodus Dioecesis Sioupolitanae, 1931 (et 1941)*, p. 5; *Quartum Concilium Provinciale Portlandensis, Acta et Decreta*, no. 80.

meetings as to whether it be a grave or a light one can be deduced from the object or end of the law and from the sanction invoked by the Code of Canon Law for non-attendance at the same conferences.[10] In considering the end, object and sanction of the law, one must conclude that there exists a grave obligation to hold the conferences. Primarily, the obligation of convening the meetings rests upon the local ordinary and the rural dean.[11] The omission of convening the conferences over a considerable length of time would constitute grave negligence. If the local ordinary judges that he cannot convene the conferences by reason of territorial circumstances, he still has a grave obligation to resort to the alternative given in the law, namely, written solutions are to be demanded of all who would otherwise be obliged to attend the meetings.

The rural dean's obligation to gather the priests of his deanery for the conferences is subsidiary to the obligation of the local ordinary. He is to convene the conferences in his deanery on the days designated or appointed by the local ordinary.[12] He is not to call the meetings without the consent of the ordinary and is obliged to follow the regulations of the local ordinary.

The obligation of the individual priests to attend the conferences is a more complex factor. This obligation binds all secular priests unless they have previously obtained exemption from their local ordinary even if they do not have the care of souls, and also when they have not received the faculty to hear confessions.[13] In case the conferences are not held in consequence of some real difficulty, all secular priests have the same obligation to present the written solutions as determined in detail by the local ordinary.[14]

Only an express exemption granted by the local ordinary will excuse them from this obligation. All priests religious, even though they be exempt are obliged to attend the conferences

[10] Canons 131 and 2377.

[11] Canons 131 and 448.

[12] Can. 448.

[13] Coronata, *Institutiones*, I, n. 190.

[14] Can. 131, § 2.

of the secular priests if they have the care of souls. The same must be said concerning religious confessors who possess diocesan faculties to hear confessions but only if they do not attend the conferences in their own houses.

The obligation of the individual priest to attend the conferences is in itself a light one, but for incidental reasons it can become grave in character not only for seculars but also for religious to whom the law applies. Non-compliance for a considerable length of time could likewise become a matter of grievous negligence. Some commentators and writers, however, maintain that the obligation is a grave or a serious one not only for confessors but also for all who are bound by law to attend the diocesan conferences.[15] There is certainly some additional reason for confessors to use the means afforded through the medium of clergy conferences for preserving and sealing their competence in the hearing of confessions. But in-as-much-as canon 2377 expressly adverts to contumacy or repeated omissions, the argument in favor of the lightness of the obligation as it attaches to the individual must still be upheld. Circumstances and scandal can, of course, make the obligation of attendance to be a grave one. The same principle would apply when written solutions are called for in place of attendance at the actual conferences.

Obligatory attendance, as a duty deriving from the universal law, came with the advent of the Church's present Code.[16] The universal law now demands attendance at the clergy conferences from those only to whom the law specifically extends. If it is difficult to convene the meetings, then the law binds the same subjects to submit answers and solutions in writing according to norms established by the local ordinary.[17] Thus the universal law demands that written solutions be handed in only if the

15 "Obligato interessendi tam pro a) [scil. pro sacerdotibus omnibus saecularibus] quam pro b) [pro Religiosis scil. exemptis curam animarum habentibus] est gravis saltem pro confessariis, ut patet ex poenis can. 2377 statutus."—Ferreres, *Compendium Theologiae Moralis* (15. ed., 2 vols., Barcinone, 1932), II, n. 920. Cf. also Galasso, *op. cit.*, p. 178.

16 Can. 131.

17 Can. 131, § 1 and § 2.

actual gatherings cannot be held, but it does not require written solutions if the individuals are excused, or if they are absent for a good reason. Particular or diocesan law can, however, oblige all who do not personally attend the conferences to submit written solutions to the chancery. Particular law can oblige even those who are present at the meetings to present written solutions. Such a measure would of course be *praeter legem* with reference to the universal law itself.

The local ordinary is the competent authority for dispensing as individual from attendance, whether the priest to be excused be a secular or a religious, even one of exempt status. It seems correct to assume that a true dispensation is contemplated in this case, even though the text of the law employs the word exemption.[18] A dispensation is a relaxation of the law in a particular case.[19] The dispensation must be given by the competent legitimate superior. In the matter concerned, the local ordinary is the proper superior even for the exempt religious who are subject to the law. It is necessary for the validity of the dispensation that it be given expressly.[20] An express dispensation can be given either explicitly or implicitly. An express dispensation which is at the same time also explicit is given in so many words; express dispensation which is at the same time only implicit is given in manifest signs, which however are no less definite in their import. A tacit or interpretative dispensation would not suffice.

The Code of Canon Law does not deal at length with the causes for a warranted dispensation from attendance at the clergy conferences. Accordingly the general norms for the granting of dispensations from ecclesiastical laws are to be followed. The dispensation certainly always postulates a just and a reasonable cause for a relaxing of the law.[21] Without the just and reasonable cause, the superior would dispense invalidly from the prescriptions of the Code of Canon Law. However, if

[18] Can. 131, § 3.

[19] Can. 80.

[20] "Conventui interesse . . . debent, nisi a loci Ordinario exemptionem ante a expresse obtinuerint."—Can. 131, § 3.

[21] "A lege ecclesiastica ne dispensetur sine iusta et rationabili causa, habita ratione gravitatis legis a qua dispensatur . . . ."—Can. 84, § 1.

the local ordinary would dispense from his own particular prescription, e.g., from the demanded written solutions over and above the duty of attendance, without a just and reasonable cause, then the dispensation would still be valid in spite of the illicit manner in which it was granted.[22] In doubt about the sufficiency of the cause, the dispensation can be licitly sought and the ordinary can validly and licitly grant it.[23]

Customs which had arisen in some localities before the promulgation of the Code of Canon Law, in regard to attendance at the clergy conferences and then, with the advent of the Code, become contrary or opposed to the present universal law must be dealt with in accord with the ruling enacted in canon 5. According to this ruling, customs, whether universal or particular, if contrary to the present universal law, must be considered as suppressed, unless the law provides otherwise. Centenary and immemorial customs alone can be tolerated, if the local ordinary finds that he cannot prudently suppress them. The law regarding attendance at the meetings makes no exception in favor of contrary local customs, and hence all customs contrary to the present universal law must be regarded as suppressed, except those centenary and immemorial customs which for prudential reasons are being tolerated by ordinaries. All former customs which in some provinces and dioceses before the present Code of Canon Law exempted canonists, golden jubiliarians, etc., from attendance at the conferences can no longer be sustained, unless they be centenary and immemorial and the ordinary has judged that he cannot prudently suppress. Such toleration is possible, since canon 131 does not contain a repudiating clause which essentially outlaws all customs to the contrary. It is true that these same persons can now be excused by their ordinary, but not in virtue of the previous custom, unless it be centenary and immemorial and cannot be obliterated in a prudent manner. They must now be excused in virtue of the norms of the present law.[24]

22 Galasso, *De Cleri Collationibus,* p. 180.

23 "Dispensatio in dubio de sufficientia causae licite petitur et potest licite et valide concedi."—Can. 84, § 2.

24 Can. 131, § 3; "Die Gewaehrung von Befreiungen ist Sache des Oberhirten."—Eichmann-Moersdorf, *Lehrbuch des Kirchenrechts,* I, 269.

Where custom may have done away with the actual gatherings or where the meetings have gone into disuse for any reason, the proper superior cannot sustain the omission under any pretense whatsoever. Such a custom is completely suppressed. Therefore the conferences must be convened where before the promulgation of the Code of Canon Law they were not held, or where the holding of them had fallen into disuse. All previous usages and customs (without prejudice to centenary and immemorial customs as mentioned above) which are contrary to what is now prescribed in the universal law are completely abolished. Besides, it is warranted that an ordinary would be gravely delinquent if through his apathy the conferences would not be held, or if he did nothing to institute, restore or supply the legal substitute for the meetings. The legal substitute is the presenting of the written solutions according to norms established by the ordinary.[25] Furthermore, if the meetings are not held in some part of the diocese because of impossibility or difficulty, the law demands that the ordinary substitute the presenting of the written solutions for the priests concerned.

Article 2. The Obligation of Attendance at the Clergy Conferences

The members of the clergy who are bound by law to attend the conferences that are prescribed in canon 131, § 1 and § 3, or who in case the conferences cannot be convened must submit written solutions, are the following priests:

1) All seculars without exception;
2) such religious, even when privileged with exemption, who have the care of souls, and
3) other religious and from the local ordinary have the faculty to hear confessions, but only if they do not have the conference in their own houses.[26]

First of all, all secular priests are bound to attend the meetings. The law does not grant any exemption from attendance for any secular priests. Since the Code of Canon Law does not

[25] Can. 131, § 2.

[26] This final clause is taken from the Council of Rome (1725). Cf. *Coll. Lac.*, I, 371.

grant any express exemption for secular priests, the intent of the law includes all, regardless of age, status, dignity, or office, who are within the confines of the diocese and serving in the diocese subject to the local ordinary, e.g., the vicar general, canonists, pastors, chaplains, officials of the diocesan curia, rural deans, assistant pastors, professors in the seminary. In a word, all the secular priests of the diocese are obliged to attend the meetings. In order to be dispensed from the obligation of attendance, an express exemption must be obtained from the local ordinary.[27]

The rural dean is, of course, obliged to attendance. However, if several conferences are convened in different places within the same deanery, as may prove necessary in a large diocese, the dean is dispensed from personally attending each and every one of them, even though the meetings are held on different days, in order that he may not be overburdened, especially if he is engaged in parish work.[28] The dean must, of course, appoint a substitute, who in his name presides at the conference, and is fully responsible for the proper supervision of the meetings in the same capacity as the dean.

In an Instruction of the Sacred Consistorial Congregation to Military Ordinariates, chaplains (secular and religious) are counseled to strive to be present at the conferences or meetings which take place according to canon 131 in the dioceses in which they are stationed.[29] The Holy See undoubtedly issued these norms for the Military Vicar in its Instruction because it recognizes the permanency of the military chaplaincy as a definite and real segment of the modern *cura animarum.*[30]

A secular priest residing outside his proper diocese for a legitimate reason, e.g., for the pursuit of post-graduate studies, for the enjoyment of a vacation, for the work of teaching, etc., would be exempt from attendance at the conferences in his home diocese and also in the diocese of the actual residence. By the very fact that he lawfully resides outside of his proper diocese

27 Can. 131, § 3.

28 Augustine, *Commentary,* II, 503.

29 *AAS,* XLIII (1951), 562; *The Jurist,* XII (1952), 145. This norm is mentioned in the seventeenth number of the Instruction.

30 *The Jurist,* XII (1952), 141.

or has been sent there under obedience by his proper bishop, he is at least implicitly exempted from attendance at the conferences in his own diocese. By leaving his diocese, the secular priest still retains his proper ordinary in the diocese of his incardination. Thus he is not held to attendance at the meetings convened in another diocese unless he is actually engaged in the ministry to souls in that diocese. By service to a diocese other than his own, the secular priest must comply with the obligation of attending the meetings there. In general, the law contemplates the secular priest as fulfilling the ministry in the diocese of his incardination. If he gives his services to another diocese, then he is obligated to the conferences of that diocese.

The same obligation binds all religious, even exempt religious, who have the care of souls in the diocese of their residence. The clause of the canon, "*curam animarum habentes*", refers specifically to religious.[31] Even though the canon mentions religious without any distinction or explanation, is is clear that only priests are singled out, since in the present universal law the care of souls is entrusted only to priests.[32] Religious, even exempt religious, when they are engaged in the care of souls are absolutely bound by the obligation of attending the conferences of the diocese where they reside. Therefore, even if the monthly meetings are held in their own houses, they are still obligated to participate in the diocesan conferences or to obtain an express exemption from the local ordinary, who can rightfully deny them this exemption.[33] If they are actually present at the conferences convened in their own houses, there exists a just and reasonable cause for petitioning the local ordinary for an exemption, and he, in turn, can validly and licitly grant it.

The comprehensive meaning of the phrase, "*religiosi curam animarum habentes*", was not entirely clear until the year 1935. Until that time there were many commentators who consid-

[31] Can. 131, § 3; Oesterle, *Praelectiones*, I, 75.

[32] "Etsi in canone dicatur 'Religiosi' sine addito, planum tamen est hic non agi nisi de sacerdotibus, cum in novo jure cura animarum demandari nequeat nisi sacerdotibus."—Galasso, *De Cleri Callationibus*, p. 183.

[33] Galasso, *loc. cit.*, pp. 182 ss.

ered only such religious as having the care of souls who by law or office exercised the ministry to souls, namely pastors, and consequently excluded the assistants in parishes, rectors of missions and quasi-pastors.[34] There was, however, one author who did not exclude the assistants in parishes, etc., from subjection to the law regarding attendance at the clergy conferences.[35]

The Pontifical Commission for the Authentic Interpretation of the Code was asked whether priests religious who are catechists or assistant pastors dependent on the pastor in hospitals and other pious institutions are obliged to attend the diocesan clerical conferences. The Commission replied that religious as catechists are not obliged, but that assistant pastors and chaplains are obliged if they take the place of the pastor and assist him in the entire parochial ministry.[36] According to this authentic response, all the priests who are exempt or non-exempt religious are obligated to attend the conferences of the secular clergy if they are assistants or chaplains dependent upon the pastor in hospitals and other pious institutions, and in accord with the norm of canon 476, § 6, supply the place of the pastor and assist him in the entire parochial ministry.

Assistant pastors are always to be included under the law here in question.[37] Their very task is to assist the pastor in the entire parochial ministry. Also religious as chaplains are considered as having the care of souls, if in hospitals and other religious institutions, etc., besides having the power to exercise sacred functions, they have the care of souls by taking the place of the pastor and assist him in the ministry. This norm is not applicable for religious who are the chaplains of religious houses, schools, etc., which are exempt by law or freed by the

[34] Goyeneche *Iuris Canonicio Summa Principia,* II, 272; T. Schaefer, *Compendium de Religiosis* (Muenster 1927), p. 379; Vermeersch, *Epitome,* I, n. 250.

[35] Oesterle, *op. cit.,* I, 75.

[36] *AAS,* XXVII (1935), 92; Bouscaren, *Canon Law Digest,* II, 53.

[37] "Eius iura et obligationes ex statutis dioecesanis, ex litteris Ordinarii et ex ipsius parochi commissione desumantur; sed, nisi aliud expresse caveatur, ipse debet ratione officii parochi vicem supplere eumque adiuvare in universo paroeciali ministerio, excepta applicatione Missae pro populo."—Can. 476, § 6.

ordinary from all dependence upon the pastor. Such chaplains cannot be considered to take the place of the pastor according to the norm of canon 476, § 6.[38] The same cannot be said for religious as the rectors of seminaries. They must be included under the law of attendance since they exercise the care of souls by reason of canon 1368 in the capacity of a pastor.

Other priests religious certainly included as exercising the care of souls are pastors and quasi-pastors,[39] acting vicars (*vicarii actuales*),[40] *vicarii oeconomi*, commonly called administrators,[41] substitute vicars (*vicarii substituti*),[42] and adjutant vicars (*vicarii adiutores*), if they supply the place of the pastor at least in the greater part of the ministry to souls.[43]

The obligation of attendance at the diocesan clergy conferences binds all religious who from the local ordinary, have the faculty to hear confessions, if they do not attend the conferences in their own houses.[44] The religious here considered are not obliged in an absolute manner, as is the case when they exercise the care of souls. The members of the clergy here included are bound only under the condition that they do not attend the conferences held in their own houses.[45] Hence it is evident that the local ordinary cannot make the attendance at his diocesan conferences a condition for granting the faculties to hear confessions, nor can he command that they be obliged to attend the diocesan meetings if they attend the conferences in their own houses according to norm of canon 591. Such a provision would be contrary to the law.[46]

38 Maroto, "De Collationibus", *Commentarium pro Religiosis*, XVI (1935), 222; Galasso, *op. cit.*, p. 185.

39 Can. 451, § 1; § 2, n. 1.

40 Can. 471, § 1.

41 Can. 473, § 1.

42 Can. 474.

43 Can. 475; Maroto, "art. cit.," *Commentarium pro Religiosis*, XVI (1935), 218.

44 Can. 131, § 3.

45 Can. 591.

46 Can. 131, § 3. Cf. also Galasso, *op. cit.*, p. 186.

One may raise the question whether the abovementioned religious are obliged to attend the diocesan conferences if they are resident in non-integrated religious houses (*domus non formatae*) wherein written solutions of cases are substituted for the actual monthly conferences. These written solutions would have to be called for by their constitutions or by their legitimate superior. In that event the demand of the law in canon 131, § 3, is fulfilled by means of the written solutions, so that the religious concerned would not have to attend the diocesan conferences. The law demands that the conferences be attended in their own houses if these religious are to be exempted from the diocesan conferences. The Code of Canon Law itself allows the substitution of written answers for the actual diocesan conferences if it is difficult to convene the meetings.[47]

There certainly seems to be good reason to conclude that religious in non-integrated houses who are bound to submit answers in writing to their superior according to their constitutions, or in accord with the consent of their legitimate superior, need not attend the diocesan conferences. The small membership in the newly formed house may be recognized as a corresponding reason for the substituted fulfillment of the law. Thus, without prejudice to any future contrary declaration of the Pontifical Commission for the Authentic Interpretation of the Code, it can be asserted that the religious who enjoy diocesan faculties for the hearing of confessions, if they substitute written solutions for actual gatherings in their own houses, do not have to attend the conferences held in the diocese where they have received confessional faculties. The same religious cannot be penalized in accord with the norm of canon 2377, namely, with suspension from hearing the confessions of seculars, provided the substitution be authorized by the competent authority.

Exempt religious are in general freed from all obligatory attendance at the diocesan conferences except in those cases wherein the law expressly subjects them to such attendance.[48] The law cancels out the exemption of religious with reference to

[47] Can. 131, § 1.

[48] Can. 131, § 3.

attendance at the diocesan clergy conferences in the following cases:

1) Exempt religious who serve in the capacity of a pastor or who have the care of souls in accord with the norm of canon 131, § 3, and canon 631, § 1, are bound by the obligation to attend the conferences in the diocese in which they are working; these religious are bound absolutely, namely, apart from all consideration whether they attend the conferences in their own houses or not.
2) Exempt religious who have faculties from the local ordinary for hearing confessions are bound to attend the diocesan conferences, but only conditionally, that is, if they do not attend the meetings held in their own houses according to canon 591.
3) All exempt priests religious who are obliged to attend the diocesan meetings in accordance with the law must hand in their written solutions to the local ordinary in compliance with his regulations and prescriptions if the actual meetings are not held because of territorial difficulties, etc. This provision of the law is entirely new.[49]

Let it be kept in mind again that, if the holding of the conferences is supplanted with the presentation of answers in writing in the houses of exempt religious confessors with faculties of the diocese to hear confessions, they need only submit the written solutions to their religious superiors. These confessors are thereby exempted from the provisions of canon 131, namely, they are not obligated to attend the diocesan conferences, nor need they submit their answers in writing to the local ordinary if the actual meetings are not held in the diocese.[50]

A decree of the Provincial Council of Portland (1932) demands that all chaplains, whether secular or religious, are bound to attend the diocesan conferences.[51] It is true that all secular chaplains are held to attend the conferences, but it seems to be

[49] Antonius Melo, *De Exemptione Regularium* (Universitas Catholica Americae, Washingtonii, D.C., 1921), pp. 75 ss.

[50] Melo, *op. cit.*, p. 76.

[51] "Illis collationibus theologicis interesse debent etiam omnes . . . Capellani, sive sint saeculares sive religiosi."—*Acta et Decreta*, n. 81.

too inclusive for the religious chaplains. Religious, as chaplains are not bound to attendance at the conferences in the diocese unless they take the place of the pastor according to the norm of canon 476, § 6, and assist him in the entire parochial ministry. Other religious who as chaplains have diocesan faculties for the hearing of confessions must attend only if they do not attend the meetings in their own houses. A simple chaplaincy does not necessarily include the care of souls.[52]

An even less reconcilable decree is that of the Plenary Council of Poland (1936), which demands that not only secular priests and religious engaged in the care of souls are bound to attend the gatherings but also all those (secular and religious) who teach Christian doctrine in the schools, namely, catechists.[53] There is no doubt about the seculars and religious who have the care of souls, but in view of the express declaration of the Pontifical Commission for the Authentic Interpretation of the Code one cannot bind catechists to attend the conferences of the diocese. Catechists here are identified with such religious who simply teach in the schools.

It has already been stated that written solutions are by law required only when the actual gatherings cannot be held because of some difficulty and that the details of these written solutions are to be determined by the local ordinary.[54] The obligation of attendance as stated in the universal law leaves room for further additions through particular law. Such an addition would be verified if written solutions were demanded over and above the actual attendance. A diocesan ruling of this type would be a measure *praeter ius,* but not contrary to it. The local ordinary can grant exemptions from this diocesan provision as he sees fit.

The priests, secular and religious, if by law they are held to attendance at the conferences, must attend unless they are expressly exempted beforehand.[55] But a decree of a diocesan

[52] Galasso, *op. cit.,* p. 188.

[53] "Sacerdotes sive saeculares sive religiosi, qui curam animarum gerunt aut doctrinam christianam in scholis tradunt, conferentiis decanalibus interesse tenentur."—*Acta et Decreta,* no. 8, as given in Galasso, *op. cit.,* p. 188, note 2.

[54] Can. 131, § 2.

[55] Can. 131, § 3.

synod or of a provincial council which would exempt all priests from the conferences except confessors would be contrary to the very tenor of the law. There would not be a just and a reasonable cause for the exemption of all the others.

The III Plenary Council of Baltimore (1884) bound all priests, secular and religious, to attend the conferences if they were engaged in the care of souls. It also bound confessors even though they were not connected with any parish, but heard the confessions of women religious in their houses, or of the laity in public churches.[56] First of all, the stricter rule of the present universal law, which does not grant exemption to any secular priests, supplants the law of this Council of Baltimore.[57] The rule for religious, even exempt, who have the care of souls seems to be the same in both laws. However, the stricter rule of the Council in its demand that religious confessors attend the diocesan conferences, even apart from the condition now expressed in the Code of Canon Law, namely, that they have not participated in the conferences in their own houses. The prescription of the conciliar law would include religious confessors even if they attended the meetings in their own houses.[58] Since this provision of the Council restricts the right given to religious confessors who attend the meetings in their own houses, the conciliar law in this regard is obliterated in favor of the present law as outlined for these confessors in the Code of Canon Law.

Barrett seemed to overlook the fact of what is now granted in favor of religious confessors by the Code if they attend the conferences in their own houses (can. 131, § 3). He simply stated without reservation that now the stricter and more exacting law of the Code of Canon prevails, when in fact the greater demands appear incorporated in the conciliar legislation.[59]

[56] "Omnes sacerdotes, sive saeculares sive regulares, qui curam gerunt animarum, iis adsistere teneantur. Neque exemptos se esse existiment confessarii, qui quamvis certae ecclesiae non sint adscripti, confessiones tamen excipiunt religiosarum feminarum in earum domibus, aut laicorum in ecclesiis publicis."—*Acta et Decreta*, no. 191.

[57] Barrett, *A Comparative Study of the Council of Baltimore and the Code of Canon Law*, p. 46.

[58] *Acta et Decreta*, no. 191.

[59] *Op. cit.*, p. 46.

CHAPTER VIII

THE PENAL SANCTION FOR ATTENDANCE AT THE CLERGY CONFERENCES

The penal sanction invoked with reference to the conferences centers solely on the obligation of attendance. It is enunciated in canon 2377.[1] The canon states that the priests who refuse in a contumacious manner to attend the conferences as prescribed in canon 131, § 1, may be punished at the prudent discretion of the ordinary. The term *sacerdotes* refers to all priests secular, and religious, even exempt, who have the care of souls. The canon adverts also to the religious confessors who have diocesan faculties for the hearing of confessions. In virtue of canon 2377, on the supposition that they have not attended the conferences in their own houses, these confessors can be suspended from hearing the confessions of seculars for their non-attendance at the diocesan clergy conferences. Exempt religious who do not have the charge of souls nor enjoy diocesan faculties to hear confessions, cannot be compelled to attend diocesan conferences under the possible penalties of canon 2377. The law simply does not include them in regard to the diocesan clergy conferences.

It has been stated that the vicar general is included in the term *ordinarius* in the diocese. His power, however, does not comprise the inflicting of penalties unless he has obtained a special mandate.[2]

Several terms employed in the canon under discussion need further explanation. First of all, it is necessary to keep in mind that the canon presupposes that an exemption or a dispensation

[1] "Sacerdotes contra praescriptum can. 131, § 1, contumaces, Ordinarius pro suo prudenti arbitrio puniat; quod si fuerint religiosi confessarii curam animarum non gerentes, eos ab audiendis saecularium confessionibus suspendat."

[2] "Vicarius Generalis sine mandato speciali non habet potestatem infligendi poenas."—Can. 2220, § 2.

from attendance was not sought or if petitioned, at least was refused by the ordinary. Moreover, contumacy is postulated by the law before the appropriate penalties can be imposed. Contumacy in general means obstinate disregard of authority, but in penal legislation it has a technical meaning in reference to the imposition of censures. In the cases of *ferendae sententiae* censures to be inflicted upon delinquent priests for non-attendance, it is necessary that, in spite of the administered warnings implied in canon 2233, § 2,[3] they do not comply with the law. Besides, one must have warrant for the presence of a grave sin before the censure can be imposed. Thus, if a priest failed to attend the conferences for a considerable length of time, it is safe to assume that he is gravely delinquent. Contumacy is considered to have ceased when the culprit has really repented of the transgression, or at least has seriously promised to comply with the law in the future.[4] The decision regarding the number of the admonitions to be made and regarding the interval to elapse between their administration if left to the prudent discretion of the ordinary.

The penal legislation which provides a sanction for attendance at the meetings divides the members into two groups.[5] The first includes all secular priests, non-exempt religious and also all religious engaged in the charge of souls. If any of these priests

[3] "Licet id legitime constet, si agatur de infligenda censura, reus reprehendatur ac moneatur ut a contumacia recedat ad normam can. 2242, § 3, dato, si prudenti eiusdem iudicis vel Superioris arbitrio casus id ferat, congruo ad resipiscentiam tempore; contumacia persistente, censura infligi potest."

[4] Bouscaren-Ellis, *Commentary,* p. 881; Cocchi, *Commentarium,* VIII, n. 251.

[5] ". . . Poenis subiiciuntur:

α) sacerdotes cleri saecularis, sacerdotes qui societatis clericalis (c. 678) alumni sunt, et religiosi licet exempti curam animarum gerentes, qui antea exemptionem a collationibus non obtinuerint;

β) religiosi licet exempti, curam animarum non gerentes, sed confessarii, in quorum domibus huiusmodi collationes non habeantur; hi enim pro audiendis confessionibus saecularium qui ad domum religiosam non pertinent, indigent iurisdictione ab ordinario loci delegata."—Cocchi, Commentarium, VIII, n. 251.

are contumacious in their refusal to attend the diocesan conferences, they are to be punished in accord with the prudent judgment of the local ordinary.[6]

The penalties imposed should be medicinal, that is, designed primarily for the correction of the delinquent. It would be extremely difficult to prescribe the same penalty for all the delinquents collectively. The prudent discretion of the local ordinary is to dictate the punishment which redound effectively to the correction of the culprit. Considerations of persons, office and dignity, should not be overlooked but on the other hand, these considerations should not be overemphasized.

Secular priests, who are not engaged in the care of souls in any capacity whatsoever, then the decisions rendered by the Sacred Congregation of Bishops and Regulars provides the best solution. According to these responses, the local ordinary should proceed with exhortations, admonitions, warnings and reproofs rather than with ecclesiastical penalties.[7]

It is evident from the law that the ordinary is given full discretionary power to impose appropriate penalties upon secular priests, non-exempt religious and other religious if these have charge of souls in his diocese, since they are his subjects in the ministry to the faithful of the diocese.[8]

The second group includes all religious who as confessors have diocesan faculties to hear confessions. The same condition is required as in canon 131, § 3, namely, that they do not attend the conferences held in their own houses according to canon 591. Contumacy again is postulated as a necessary supposition for the imposing of the determined penalty, i.e., suspension from hearing the confessions of seculars. Since penalties are always to be interpreted strictly or narrowly,[9] that is, in such a manner

[6] Can. 2377.

[7] S. C. Ep. et. Reg., 23 aug., 1593; also of 13 nov., 1593, as referred to by Augustine, *Commentary,* VIII, p. 456, note 1; *Supra,* p. 10.

[8] "In omnibus in quibus religiosi subsunt Ordinario loci, possunt ab eodem etiam poenis coerceri."—can. 619.

[9] "Leges quae poenam statuunt . . . strictae subsunt interpretationi."—can. 19.

that in the face of any real doubt their applicability is to be minimized rather than magnified, the following religious in their capacity of confessors could not be penalized:

a) Those who are excused from attending the meetings held in their own houses, provided the reason for their exemption be not the fact that they are confessors in the diocese, and
b) those for whom the community's competent superior has substituted solutions in writing to take the place of the actual meetings.

Suspension from hearing the confessions of seculars does not include seculars attached to exempt religious houses. For instance, if the local ordinary suspenses an exempt religious confessor in regard to the diocesan faculties, the same religious is not suspended from hearing the confessions of the seculars attached to the religious house.[10]

The penalty of suspension from hearing the confessions of seculars is the sole penalty to be imposed upon the religious who hold confessional jurisdiction in the diocese and therefore is also the maximum penalty. For example, the suspension from the celebration of Holy Mass could not be imposed upon a religious enjoying diocesan faculties to hear confessions if he is gravely delinquent relative to his obligation of attendance at the diocesan clergy conferences. The religious mentioned here are subject to the local ordinary in so far as they have received diocesan faculties to hear confessions of seculars. In turn, the local ordinary is permitted by law to deprive them of the diocesan confessional faculties if they do not comply with the obligation of attendance at the conferences. The same penalty was established in the Council of Rome (1725) for contumacious religious if they served as confessors in a diocese.[11]

Father Galasso gives several reasons why the local ordinary is allowed to suspend religious from hearing simply the confessions

[10] Cocchi, *loc. cit.*

[11] *Coll. Lac.*, III, cols. 371, 435 ss. There is, however, some change in regard to the penalties for secular priests. The Council referred only to fines, whereas the Code of Canon Law suggests other and more stringent penalties of an indeterminate character.

of seculars,[12] for otherwise the local ordinary would involve himself in the general discipline and internal government of religious. Furthermore, it could well happen that some community would be deprived of the celebration of the Mass, if the religious as confessor were also suspended from saying Mass. Again, a religious superior could be called upon to pay a fine as imposed for non-attendance of one of his subjects at the diocesan conferences, but since the very purpose of the infliction of the penalty is the correction of the individual, such an imposed fine would rather touch the community and not the individual. The very import of the penalty would be frustrated.[13]

The penalties more frequently imposed upon delinquents for non-attendance at the meetings can be classified in three separate groups. The following are found in the provisions of European synods and councils:

1) Fines—the proceeds of which redound to the local seminary.
2) Suspension (sometimes incurred *ipso facto*) from the celebration of Holy Mass; suspension from preaching in the diocese, or the loss of diocesan faculties.
3) More serious penalties if reform is not forthcoming after the infliction of the above-mentioned penalties.[14]

The present writer, in perusing the diocesan legislation of archdioceses and dioceses in the United States, has been unable to discover any determined penalties listed for delinquent non-attendance at the conferences. The particular legislation in our country merely restates the norm of the Code, namely, that the punishment of culprits in regard to the obligation of attendance at the meetings is left to the discretion of the local ordinary.

The III Plenary Council of Baltimore (1884) stated briefly that the priests who frequently neglected their obligation to attend the meetings without legitimate excuse of permission of the ordinary should be punished.[15] The provision of the Council

[12] *De Cleri Collationibus*, p. 196.

[13] *Op. cit.*, pp. 195-196.

[14] Galasso, *op. cit.*, p. 197.

[15] "Qui absque legitimo impedimento et Ordinarii venia adesse saepius neglexerint, puniantur."—*Acta et Decreta*, no. 191.

was not as inclusive as the law of the present Code of Canon Law since it did not include all secular priests but only those who were engaged in the charge or care of souls.[16] The present law of the Code which is more inclusive than the conciliar law must prevail.[17]

The Council with references to religious who held diocesan confessional faculties, made no distinction between those who had or those who had not attended the meetings in their own houses.[18] All were simply obliged to attend the diocesan conferences. The Code of Canon Law directly states that the religious, even as confessors, who attend the conferences in their own houses are exempt from attendance at the diocesan conferences. Thus the more stringent law of the Council is opposed to the Code of Canon Law and accordingly is abrogated. Furthermore, since the present Code designates the penalty for delinquent confessors religious who do not attend the meetings in their own houses, this new determinate provision supplants the indeterminate penalties suggested in the legislation of the Council.[19]

Finally, in regard to the possible penalties for non-compliance with the obligation to attend the conferences, it will be wholesome to recall the wording of the initial canon on penalties, which reflects the Church's mind and the spirit of the law in this matter.[20] The present Code of Canon Law reiterates the senti-

16 "Omnes sacerdotes, sive saeculares sive regulares, qui curam gerunt animarum, iis adsistere teneantur."—*Acta et Decreta,* no. 191.

17 Barrett, *A Comparative Study of the Councils of Baltimore and the Code of Canon Law,* p. 46.

18 "Neque exemptos se esse existiment confessarii, qui quamvis certae ecclesiae non sint adscripti, confessiones tamen excipiunt religiosarum feminarum in earum domibus, aut laicorum in ecclesiis publicis."—*Acta et Decreta,* no. 191.

19 "Qui absque legitimo impedimento et Ordinarii venia adesse saepius neglexerint, puniantur."—*Acta et Decreta,* no. 191.

20 "Prae oculis autem habeatur monitum Conc. Trid., sess. XIII, *de ref., cap. 1:* 'Meminerint Episcopi aliique Ordinarii se pastores non percussores esse, atque ita praeesse sibi subditis oportere, ut non in eis dominentur, sed illos tanquam filios et fratres diligant elaborentque ut hortando et monendo ab illicitis deterreant, ne ubi deliquerint, debitis eos poenis coercere cogantur; quos tamen si quid per humanam fragilitatem peccare

ments of the legislators at the Council of Trent, namely, that Ordinaries should be mindful of the fact that frequently benevolence is better than austerity, exhortation more persuasive than threats, charity more effective than power. Whenever punishment is necessary, so canon 2214, § 2, continues, rigor should be tempered with gentleness, judgment with mercy, and severity with clemency.

---

contigerit, illa Apostoli est ab eis servanda praeceptio ut illos arguant, obsecrent, increpent in omni bonitate et patientia, cum saepe plus erga corrigendos agat benevolentia quam austeritas, plus exhortatio quam comminatio, plus caritas quam potestas; sin autem ob delicti gravitatem virga opus erit, tunc cum mansuetudine rigor, cum misericordia iudicium, cum lenitate severitas adhibenda est, us since asperitate disciplina, populis salturaris ac necessaria, conservetur et qui correcti fuerint, emendentur, aut, si resipiscere noluerint, ceteri, salubri in eos animadversionis exemplo, a vitiis deterreantur ' "—Can. 2214, § 2.

CONCLUSIONS

1. There is proof that clergy conferences were conducted with some degree of regularity as early as the fourth century. Saint Charles Borromeo introduced the conferences into Italy, but the opinion that under the impetus of his action all other dioceses adopted the practice is not supported by historical evidence.

2. Clergy conferences were of frequent occurrence as early as the sixth century under the name of synods.

3. Piety, zeal for souls and the love of sacred learning were fostered through the medium of the conferences in certain periods of the Church, especially in the time of Saint Charles Borromeo and Saint Vincent de Paul.

4. Until the promulgation of the present Code as the Church's universal law, the obligation of attending the conferences derived solely through particular legislation and enactments.

5. The final object of clergy conferences is not only the preservation but also the promotion or furtherance of knowledge and piety among the clergy.

6. Since the very concept of a conference implies oral discussion, the presentations of lectures cannot be considered the equivalent of conferences in the canonical sense.

7. The necessary subject-matter of the conferences as determined in law deals with the practical problems of moral theology and liturgy. Matters concerning other subjects which the ordinary judges conducive to the promotion of knowledge and piety among his clergy are entirely within his discretion. The law does not determine these matters.

8. The III Plenary Council of Baltimore allowed topics in dogmatic theology to form part of the necessary subject-matter of the conferences (*Acta et Decreta,* no. 192). This law of the Council must yield to the change which the present universal law has introduced.

9. The III Plenary Council of Baltimore prescribed at least four conferences each year in the cities, and two each year in the

rural districts (*Acta et Decreta,* no. 192). This enactment still remains as a suitable determination of the law of the Code of Canon Law.

10. In the light of adverse circumstances and territorial difficulties, the holding of the conferences twice a year could actually fulfill the "*saepius in anno*" prescriptions of canon 131. In this case, then, written solutions would not have to be demanded in place of any additional conferences that cannot be held.

11. Legitimate custom seems to warrant the non-presentation of the solution of a case of conscience, as had been prescribed in the III Plenary Council of Baltimore (*Acta et Decreta,* no. 192).

12. The obligation of convening the conferences, or of substituting written solutions if the actual gatherings cannot be held, is a grave one, and for its performance and fulfillment the local ordinary and the rural dean share responsibility.

13. The obligation of the individual to attend the conferences is in itself not a grave one, but a deliberate and inexcusable non-attendance for a considerable length of time would constitute grave negligence, which in turn renders the individual liable for the penalties enacted in canon 2377.

14. Suspension from hearing the confessions of seculars is the sole and the maximum penalty which can be imposed upon religious who have diocesan confessional faculties when they have failed to attend the conferences in their own religious houses.

BIBLIOGRAPHY

Sources

Acta Apostolicae Sedis, Commentarium Officiale, Romae, 1909-1929; Civitate Vaticana, 1929-

Acta Ecclesiae Mediolanensis, a Sancto Carolo Cardinali S. Praxedis Archi. Mediolan. Condita, Frederici Cardinalis Borromaei Archiepiscopi Mediolan. iussu undique diligentius collecta, et edita, 2 vols., Lugduni, 1682-1683. Tom. I, 1682; Tom. II, 1683.

Acta et Decreta Concilii Plenarii Baltimorensis Tertii A.D. MDCCCLXXXIV, Baltimore: Typis Joannie Murphy Sociarum, 1886.

Acta et Decreta Sacrorum Conciliorum Recentium, Collectio Lacensis, 7 vols., Friburgi Brisgoviae, 1870-1892.

Acta Sanctae Sedis, 41 vols., Romae, 1865-1908.

Bail, L., *Summa Conciliorum,* (2 vols., Padova, 1723).

Bouscaren, T. Lincoln, *The Canon Law Digest,* 3 vols., Vol. I, 4. printing, 1934; Vol. II, 1943, Vol. III, 1954, Milwaukee, Wis.: The Bruce Publishing Co., Supplements for 1953, 1954 and 1955 in 1954, 1955, and 1956.

Bruns, Hermann, *Canones Apostolorum et Conciliorum Saeculorum IV-VII,* 2 vols., Berolini, 1839.

Codex Iuris Canonici Pii X Pontificis Maximi iussu digestus, Benedicti Papae XV auctoritate promulgatus, Praefatione, Fontium Annotatione et Indice Analytico-Alphabetico ab Emo Petro Card. Gasparri Auctus, Romae: Typis Polyglottis Vaticanis, 1917; reimpressio, 1934.

Codicis Iuris Canonici Fontes, cura Emi Petri Card. Gasparri editi, 9 vols., Romae (postea Civitate Vaticana): Typis Polyglottis Vaticanis, 1923-1939. (Vols. VII-IX, ed. cura et studio Emi Iustiniani Card. Serédi).

Concilia Germaniae, auctore et auspice Joanne F. Schannat, primo collegit Josephus Hartzheim, continuavit et prelo dedit P. Hermannus Scholl, 11 vols., Vols. I-X, Coloniae Augustae Agrippinensium, 1759-1775; Vol. XI, Indice, opera et studio Amandi J. Hesselmann, 1790.

Concilia Provincialia Baltimori Habita ab anno MDCCCXXIX usque ad annum MDCCCXLIX, 2. ed. Baltimore: John Murphy, 1851.

Concilium Plenarium Totius Americae Septentrionalis Foederatae Baltimori Habitum A.D. MDCCCLII, Baltimore: John Murphy, 1853.

Concilium Romanum in Sacrosancta Basilica Lateranensi celebratum anno 1725, Romae, 1725.

Decretales D. Gregorii Papae IX, suae integritati una cum glossis restitutae, cum privilegio Gregorii XIII, Pont. Max., et Aliorum Principum, Romae, 1582.

Hardouin, Jean, *Acta Conciliorum et Epistolae Decretales ac Constitutiones Summorum Pontificum,* 12 vols., Parisiis, 1714-1715.

Jaffé, Philippus, *Regesta Pontificum Romanorum ab condita Ecclesia ad annum post Christum natum MCXCVIII,* ed. 2. correctam et auctam auspiciis G. Wattenbach curaverunt F. Kaltenbrunner, P. Ewald, S. Loewenfeld, 2 vols., Lipsiae, 1885-1888.

Liber Sextus Decretalium D. Bonifacii Papae VIII, suae integritati cum Clementis et Extravagantibus, earumque Glossis restitutis, Romae, 1582.

Mansi, Joannes, *Sacrorum Conciliorum Nova et Amplissima Collectio,* 53 vols. in 60, Parisiis, 1901-1927.

Potthast, Augustus, *Regesta Pontificum Romanorum inde ab anno post Christum natum MCXCVIII ad annum MCCCIV,* 2 vols., Berolini, 1874-1875.

Synods—

Synodus Diocesana Brooklyniensis Quinta (1926).

Eighth Synod of Dubuque (1947) Statutes of the Archdiocese of Dubuque.

Synodus Dioecesana Eriensis Septima (1942), Acta et Decreta.

The Third Synod of Nashville (1947), Acts and Decrees.

Acta et Decreta Concilii Provincialis Portlandensis in Oregon Quarti (MCMXXXII).

First Synod of Scranton (1949).

Synodus Dioecesana Sioupolitana Quarta (1931).

Synodus Dioecesana Sioupolitana Quinta (1941).

Reference Works

Abbo, John A.—Hannan, Jerome D., *The Sacred Canons,* 2 vols., St. Louis: B. Herder Book Co., 1952.

Antonelli, Joannes, *De Iuribus et Oneribus Clericorum,* Romae, 1699.

Augustine, Charles, *A Commentary on the New Code of Canon Law,* 8 vols., Vol. I, 3. ed., 1920; Vol. II, 3. ed., 1919; Vol. III, 2. ed., 1919, St. Louis: B. Herder Book Co.

———, *Liturgical Law,* St. Louis and London: B. Herder Book Co., 1931.

Badii, Cesar, *Institutiones Iuris Canonici,* 3. ed., 2 vols., Florentiae: Libreria Editrice Fiorentina, 1921-1922.

Barbosa, Augustinus, *Iuris Ecclesiastici Universi Libri III,* 3 vols. in 2, Lugduni, 1660.

Barrett, John, *A Comparative Study of the Councils of Baltimore and the Code of Canon Law,* The Catholic University of America Canon Law Studies, n. 83, Washington D. C.: The Catholic University of America, 1932.

Benedictus XIV (Prospero Lambertini), *De Synodo Dioecesana,* 2. ed., 4 vols., Mechlinae, 1842.

Berutti, Christophorus, *Institutiones Iuris Canonici,* 6 vols., Vol. II, Pars I, 1943; Vol. VI, 1938, Taurini-Romae: Marietti.

Beste, A., *Introductio in Codicem,* 3. ed., Collegeville, Minn.: St. John's Abbey Press, 1946.

Blat, Albertus, *Commentarium Textus Codicis Iuris Canonici,* 5 vols. in 7, Vol. II, Pars 1, *De Personis,* 2. ed., 1921; Vol. V, 1924, Romae: Collegio Angelico.

Bouix, Dominicus, *Tractatus de Episcopo,* 2. ed., 2 vols. in 1, Parisiis, 1873.

Bouscaren, T. Lincoln—Ellis, Adam C., *Canon Law, A Text and Commentary,* 2. printing, Milwaukee, Wis.: The Bruce Publishing Co., 1948.

Busquet, Josephus—Garcia-Bayon, Jesus, *Thesaurus Confessarii,* 10. ed., Matriti, 1940.

Cappello, Felix, *Summa Iuris Canonici,* 3 vols., Vol. I, 4. ed., Romae: Apud Aedes Universitatis Gregorianae, 1945.

Chelodi, Ioannes, *Ius Canonicum de Delictis et Poenis,* 5. ed., recognita et aucta a Pio Ciprotti, Vicenza: Società Anonima Tipografica; Trento: A. Ardesi, 1943.

———, *Ius Canonicum de Personis,* 3. ed., curavit Pius Ciprotti, Vicenza: Società Anonima Tipografica: Trento: A. Ardesi, 1942.

Cicognani, Amleto G., *Canon Law,* 2. ed., Westminster, Md.: The Newman Press, 1947.

Cocchi, Guidus, *Commentarium in Codicem Iuris Canonici,* 8 vols., Vol. I, 6. ed., 1947; Vol. II, 4. ed., 1937; Vol. IV, 4. ed., 1946; Vol. VIII, 4. ed., 1938, Taurinorum Augustae: Marietti.

Coronata, Matthaeus Conte a, *Institutiones Iuris Canonici,* 5 vols., Vol. I, 4. ed., 1950; Vol. II, 3. ed., 1947, Romae: Marietti.

Coste, Pierre, *Life and Labours of Saint Vincent de Paul,* translated by Joseph Leonard, 3 vols., London, 1934-1935.

———, *The Life and Works of Saint Vincent de Paul,* 3 vols., Westminster, Md.: The Newman Press, 1952.

Davis, Henry, *Moral and Pastoral Theology,* 6. ed., 4 vols., London-New York: Sheed and Ward, 1949.

De Angelis, Phillipus, *Praelectiones Iuris Canonici,* 5 vols. in 9, Romae: Ex Typographia della Pace; Parisiis: Apud P. Lethielleux, 1877-1891.

De Meester, Alphonsus, *Iuris Canonici et Iuris Canonico-Civilis Compendium,* 4 vols., Vol. I, nova. ed., Brugis: Sumptibus et Typis Societatis Sancti Augustini, 1921.

Eichmann, E.-Moersdorf, K., *Lehrbuch des Kirchenrechts auf Grund des Codex Iuris Canonici,* 6. ed., 3 vols., Paderborn: Schoeningh, 1949-1950.

Feine, H., *Kirchliche Rechtsgeschichte,* 2 vols. (Vol. I, 1950), Weimar: Herman Boehlaus Nachfolger, 1950-

Ferreres, Juan, *Institutiones Canònicas,* 2 vols. (Tom. I, 1926), Barcellona, 1926.

Galasso, Silvester, *De Cleri Collationibus,* Potentiae: Marinnucci, 1940.

Genicot, Ed.-Salsmans, I., *Institutiones Theologiae Moralis,* ed., 2 vols., Bruxelles: A. Dewit, 1927.

Goyeneche, S., *Iuris Canonici Summa Principia,* Romae, 1935.

Greco, P., *Compendio di Sacra Liturgica* (Lecco, 1922).

Hoffmann, Alexius, *Liturgical Dictionary,* Collegeville, Minn.: Liturgical Press, 1928.

Jone, Heribertus, *Commentarium in Codicem Iuris Canonici,* 3 vols., Paderborn: Officina Libraria F. Schöningh, 1950-1955.

Leitner, M., *Handbuch des katholischen Kirchenrechts,* 5 Lieferungen in 2 Bände Regensburg, 1918-1927.

Maroto, Philippus, *Institutiones Iuris Canonici,* 2 vols., Vol. I, 3. ed., Romae: Apud Commentarium pro Religiosis, 1921.

Melo, Antonius, *De Exemptione Regularium,* Universitas Catholica Americae, Washingtonii, D. C., 1921.

Michiels, Gommarus, *Normae Generales Iuris Canonici, Commentarius Libri I Codicis Iuris Canonici,* 2 vols., Vol. I, Lublin, Polonia: Universitas Catholica, 1929; Vol. II, 2. ed., Parisiis-Tournaci-Romae: Desclée et Socii, 1949.

Migne, J. P., *Patrologiae Cursus Completus, Series Greaeca,* 161 vols., Parisiis, 1857-1866.

———, *Patrologiae Cursus Completus, Series Latina,* 221 vols., Parisiis, 1844-1855.

Noldin, H.-Schmitt, A., *Summa Theologiae Moralis,* 3 vols., 26. ed., Oeniponte/Lipsiae: Rauch, 1940.

Oesterle, Gerardus, *Praelectiones Iuris Canonici,* Vol. I, Romae, 1931.

Ojetti, Benedictus, *Commentarium in Codicem Iuris Canonici,* 4 vols., Romae: Apud Aedes Universitatis Gregorianae, 1927-1931.

Ploechl, Willibald, M., *Geschichte des Kirchenrechts,* 2 Bände, Wien-Muenchen: Verlag Herold, 1953-1955.

Pruemmer, Dominicus, *Manuale Theologiae Morelis,* 8. ed., 3 vols., Friburgi-Brisgoviae: Herder & Co., 1935-1936.

Ramstein, Matthew, *A Manual of Canon Law,* Hoboken, N. J.: Terminal Printing and Publishing Co., 1947.

Roelker, Edward, *Invalidating Laws,* Paterson, N. J.: St. Anthony Guild Press, 1955.

Ryan, Gerald, *Principles of Episcopal Jurisdiction,* The Catholic University of America Canon Law Studies, n. 120, Washington, D. C.: The Catholic University of America Press, 1939.

Schaefer, Timotheus, *De Religiosis ad Normam Codicis Iuris Canonici,* editio quarta aucta et emendata, Romae: Typis Polyglottis Vaticanis, 1947.

Schmalzgrueber, Franciscus, *Ius Ecclesiasticum Universum,* 5 vols. in 12, Romae, 1843-1845.

Sipos, Stephanus, *Enchiridion Iuris Canonici,* Pecs: Ex Typographia "Haladas R. T.", 1926.

Smith, S. B., *Elements of Ecclesiastical Law,* 3 vols., Vol. I, 9. ed., New York-Cincinnati-Chicago: Benziger Brothers, 1887.

Thomassinus, Ludovicus, *Vetus et Nova Ecclesiae Disciplina,* 3 vols., Parisiis: apud Andream Crass, 1787.

Toso, Albertus, *Ad Codicem Iuris Canonici Commentaria Minora,* 2 libri in 5 toms., Lib. I, Romae: Tiferni Tiberini, Ex. Offic. Typogr. Vinciana, 1921; Lib. II, Tom. I, Taurini-Romae: Marietti, 1922.

Van Hove, Alphonsus, *Commentarium Lovaniense in Codicem Iuris Canonici,* 1 vol. in 5 toms., Tom. I, *Prolegomena,* 2. ed., 1945; Tom. III, *De Consuetudine,* 1933, Mechliniae-Romae: H. Dessain.

Vermeersch, A.-Creusen, J., *Epitome Iuris Canonici,* 3 vols., Vol. I, 7. ed., 1949; Vol. III, 6. ed., 1946, Mechliniae-Romae: H. Dessain.

Wernz, Franciscus Xaverius, *Ius Decretalium* 6 vols., Romae, 1898-1914.

Wernz, F. X.-Vidal, Petrus, *Ius Canonicum ad Codicis Normam Exactum,* 7 vols. in 8, Vol. II, 3. ed., Romae: Apud Aedes Universitatis Gregorianae, 1943.

Woywod, Stanislaus, *A Practical Commentary on the Code of Canon Law,* 10. printing, 2 vols., revised by Callistus Smith, New York: Joseph F. Wagner, Inc., 1946.

Zaplotnik, Joannes, *De Vicariis Foraneis,* Catholica Universitas Americae, Washingtonii, 1927.

ARTICLES

———, " Deanery Conferences ", Cases and Studies, *The Jurist,* VII (1947), 88-89.

———, " Religious and Conference Attendance ", Cases and Studies, *The Jurist,* VII (1947), 317.

———, " Written Conference Solutions ", Cases and Studies, *The Jurist,* VII (1947), 89.

Crovella, Hercules, "Annotationes ad Adhort. ' Menti Nostrae ' de sanctitate vitae Sacerdotalis, *Apollinaris,* XXIII (1950), 220-229.

Marbach, Joseph F., " The Recent Instruction of the Sacred Consistorial Congregation Regarding Military Ordinariates ", *The Jurist,* XII (1952), 141-150.

Maroto, P., " De Collationibus Moralibus ", *Commentarium pro Religiosis,* XVI (1935), 215-222.

PERIODICALS

Apollinaris, Romae, 1928-

Clergy Review, The, London, 1931-

Commentarium pro Religiosis, Romae, 1920-

Homeletic and Pastoral Review, The, New York, 1900-

Irish Ecclesiastical Record, The, Dublin, 1864-

Jurist, The, Washington, D. C., 1941-

Periodica de Religiosis et Missionariis, Brugis, 1905-1919; *Periodica de Re Canonica et Morali, utilia praesertim Religiosis et Missionariis,* Brugis, 1920-1927; *Periodica de Re Morali, Canonica, Liturgica,* Brugis, 1927-1936, Romae, 1937-

ABBREVIATIONS

AAS—*Acta Apostolicae Sedis.*
DTC—Dictionnaire de Théologie Catholique.
FONTES—Codicis Iuris Canonici Fontes, cura . . . Gasparri.
Coll. Lac.—Collectio Lacensis.
Mansi—J. D. Mansi, *Sacrorum Conciliorum Nova et Amplissima Collectio.*
MPG—(Migne, *Patrologia Graeca*) Jacques Paul Migne, *Patrologiae Cursus Completus*—Series Graeca.
MPL—(Migne, *Patrologia Latina*) Jacques Paul Migne, *Patrologiae Cursus Completus*—Series Latina.
S.C.C.—Sacra Congregatio Concilii.
S. C. Ep. et Reg.—Sacra Congregatio Episcoporum et Regularium.
Thomassinus—Ludivicus Thomassinus, *Vetus et Nova Ecclesiae Disciplina.*
Wernz-Vidal—*Ius Canonicum ad Codicis Normam Exactum.*

ALPHABETICAL INDEX

BIOGRAPHICAL NOTE

Lawrence Joseph Hoffman was born on September 7, 1926, in Carroll, Iowa. He received his grammar school education at Holy Angels' parochial school at Roselle, Iowa, and his high school education at St. Paul Preparatory Seminary at Epworth, Iowa. After completing his college course at St. Mary's Seminary, Techny, Ill., he entered St. Mary of the Lake Seminary in Mundelein, Ill. From this institution he received the Bachelor of Arts degree in 1951 and the Baccalaureate in Theology the following year. He was ordained to the Holy Priesthood on May 5, 1954, for the Diocese of Sioux City, Iowa. In September of the same year he enrolled in the School of Canon Law of the Catholic University, where he received the Baccalaurete in Canon Law in June of 1955, and the Licentiate in Canon Law in June of 1956.

CANON LAW STUDIES *

No. 375. Kelleher, Rev. Francis T., A.B., J.C.L., Judicial expenses.

No. 376. Bantigue, Rev. Pedro N., J.C.L., The Provincial Council of Manila of 1771.
(Its text followed by a commentary on *Actio II, De Episcopis*).

No. 377. Burns, Rev. Dennis J., J.C.L., Matrimonial indissolubility: contrary conditions.

No. 378. Deutsch, Rev. Bernard F., J.C.L., Jurisdiction of pastors in the external forum.

No. 379. Dunnivan, Rev. John P., A.B., J.C.L., Prejudicial attempts in pending litigation.

No. 380. Ernst, Rev. Albert C., A.B., J.C.L., Free admission to church for sacred rites.

No. 381. Frattin, Peter Louis, J.C.L., The matrimonial impediment of impotence: occlusion of the spermatic ducts and vaginismus.

No. 382. Henry, Rev. Charles W., O.S.B., A.B., S.T.L., J.C.L., Canonical relations between bishops and abbots at the beginning of the tenth century.

No. 383. Hoffman, Rev. Lawrence J., A.B., S.T.B., J.C.L., Clergy Conferences: Canon 131.

No. 384. Markham, Rev. James J., A.B., S.T.L., J.C.L., The Sacred Congregation of Seminaries and Universities of Studies.

No. 385. McGrath, Rev. John J., A.B., LL.B., J.C.L., A comparative study of crime and its imputability in ecclesiastical criminal law and in American criminal law.

No. 386. McGuire, Rev. James D., O.R.S.A., J.C.L., The postulancy.

No. 387. Munday, Rev. James E., J.C.L., Ecclesiastical Property in Australia and New Zealand.

No. 388. Murphy, Rev. Joseph P., A.B., J.C.L., The laws of the State of New York affecting church property.

No. 389. Pickard, Rev. Wm. M., J.C.L., Judicial experts: a source of evidence in ecclesiastical trials.

No. 390. Ruddy, Rev. James, J.C.L., The Apostolic Constitution *Christus Dominus:* text, translation and commentary, with short annotations on the Motu Proprio *Sacram Communionem.*

No. 391. Vanyo, Rev. Leo V., A.B., J.C.L., Requisites of intention in the reception of the sacraments.

* For a complete list of the available numbers of this series apply to the Catholic University of America Press, 620 Michigan Avenue, N.E., Washington (17), D. C., for a general catalog.

www.ingramcontent.com/pod-product-compliance
Lightning Source LLC
LaVergne TN
LVHW050201080826
844660LV00012B/326

* 9 7 8 0 8 1 3 2 2 5 4 3 2 *